החדש הזה לכם
ה'ש"ת

CREATION
AND
REDEMPTION

החדש הזה לכם
ה'ש"ת

CREATION
AND
REDEMPTION

a chasidic discourse by
Rabbi Yosef Yitzchak Schneersohn
זצוקללה"ה נבג"מ זי"ע
of Lubavitch

•

translation and annotation by
Rabbi Yosef Marcus

additional annotation by
Rabbi Ari Sollish

KEHOT PUBLICATION SOCIETY
770 Eastern Parkway / Brooklyn, New York 11213

CREATION AND REDEMPTION

Published and Copyrighted © 2007
by
KEHOT PUBLICATION SOCIETY
770 Eastern Parkway / Brooklyn, New York 11213
(718) 774-4000 / Fax (718) 774-2718

Orders:
291 Kingston Avenue / Brooklyn, New York 11213
(718) 778-0226 / Fax (718) 778-4148
www.kehotonline.com

ISBN: 978-0-8266-0744-7

Manufactured in the United States of America

CONTENTS

ב"ה

PREFACE

We hereby present *Creation and Redemption*, a discourse delivered by the sixth Lubavitcher Rebbe, Rabbi Yosef Yitzchak Schneersohn. This discourse, one of the first authored by Rabbi Yosef Yitzchak when he arrived in America in 5700 (1940), examines the essential difference between the Hebrew months of Tishrei and Nissan, and the mystical dimensions each represents.

In the month of Tishrei we celebrate the miracle of Creation with Rosh Hashanah, the day that commemorates the birth of the world. Creation, however, is indicative of the natural order. The month of Nissan, in contrast, during which we commemorate the miraculous Exodus from Egypt, represents Redemption, or the supernatural.

These two forces exist not only within the world at large, and within the perpetual cycle of time, but they exist within each of us as well. Each of us has moments when we feel trapped within our natural, materialistic lives, when we cannot hear the voice of our own souls amidst the deafening thunder of the daily grind. Then, there are other moments, tranquil oases in time, when we experience spiritual clarity, when we perceive a higher, deeper, more meaningful Truth.

The key, then, when struggling with the obfuscation of the natural and materialistic, is to recognize that there is another dimension, a deeper dimension, where the limitations of the natural order do not exist. Nissan is the month when we were liberated from slavery to the world's superpower in a completely supernatural manner. To this Nissan-realm, there are no limitations, nothing to stand in the way of spiritual fulfillment. In fact, the physical exists only so that we may demonstrate how it too exposes the Divine truth. And when we recognize this, says Rabbi Yosef Yitzchak, we can realize the supernatural even within the natural.

* * *

The discourse, which opens with the verse (Exodus 12:2), *This month is for you the first of months; it is, for you, the first of the months of the year*, was originally published in Hebrew in 5711 (1951) as part of a collection of discourses delivered in the summer of 5700 (1940). It appears here in English for the first time.

In this edition, we have included three appendices that further develop certain topics discussed in the discourse. These are titled *The Letters of Creation, Creation Vs. Splitting of the Sea* and *Malchut and the Other Sefirot*. The first two appendices contain selected chapters from Rabbi Schneur Zalman of Liadi's *Shaar Hayichud Veha'emunah*, which were adapted from *Lesson in Tanya* (Kehot, 1989).

The discourse was translated and annotated by Rabbi Yosef Marcus. Additional annotation was provided by Rabbi Ari Sollish. Special thanks are due to Rabbis Avraham D. Vaisfiche, Dovid Olidort and Yosef B. Friedman for their editorial guidance.

Kehot Publication Society

12 Menachem Av 5766

RABBI YOSEF YITZCHAK SCHNEERSOHN
זצוקללה"ה נבג"מ זי"ע
5640-5710 (1880-1950)

Facsimile of the original manuscript of the first discourse delivered
by Rabbi Yosef Yitzchak Schneersohn, sixth Lubavitcher Rebbe,
upon assuming the mantle of leadership in Nissan 5680 (1920)

INTRODUCTION
AND
SUMMARY

INTRODUCTION AND SUMMARY

Tuesday, nineteenth of March, 1940. The Swedish liner Drottingholm sits docked at the New York harbor. On board, among the other 800 or so passengers, sits a sixty-year-old man in a wheelchair. He is approached by the captain and asked whether he would prefer to be first or last to embark. He chooses the latter.

His name is Rabbi Yosef Yitzchak Schneersohn, and he is the sixth Rebbe of the Chabad-Lubavitch dynasty. It is the second time he has come to United States of America. The first time, in 1929, he had come to visit. This time, he has come to stay.

He sees his migration to the Western Hemisphere as fulfilling a Divine dictate: to bring Judaism and Chasidism to American soil—a soil that has until now proved inhospitable to the survival of Judaism.

Even his supporters are skeptical. "Not here," they say kindly, "not in America. America is different." But the Rebbe, who had stood down the Communists and escaped the Nazis, is not easily daunted—not even by sophisticates with top hats, bow ties and patronizing smiles.

There are some Jews living in America who are righteous—but they are completely apathetic to the spiritual malady plaguing their country, content instead to lead their lives undisturbed.

The Rebbe has no such intentions. He is not about to ignore his surroundings. He plans to light a spiritual fire, one luminous enough to bring light to the entire world.

"America is not different," he declares. *America iz nit andersh.*

Not that he is oblivious to the challenge. Even among his own Chasidim he sees a troubling shift. In his diary he writes about contemplating "the vast difference between Lubavitch in Lubavitch and Lubavitch in New York." He describes the rich, spiritual life of the olden days and the focus on spiritual matters.

"And now, what? Lubavitch of New York. It is difficult for me to write of this, for my heart is greatly pained."

The pain of his heart notwithstanding, the Rebbe immediately begins to act. He sees that while the American Jews have built beautiful synagogues, they have failed to build Jewish schools. By 1942, several Jewish day schools under his direction dot the country. He opens a publishing house that produces authentically Jewish educational materials in English, an uncommon phenomenon at the time. Despite being a brilliant Torah scholar and a profound mystic, he is involved in such non-glorious activities as ensuring that Jewish children be able to recognize an *alef* from a *bet*.

Yet he sees himself primarily as a teacher of Chasidism. In late summer 1939, he commented to Rabbi Yisroel Jacobson[1]:

> "Those who were active in the movement to arrange my moving to America after my first visit there considered it as a community undertaking (i.e., that I come as a leader of Jewry). But that is not my exclusive work, although I have been successful at it. A special concern of mine is Chasidim and Chasidus...."[2]

Less than a month after his arrival, the Rebbe had already authored three profound Chasidic discourses—one of which is the present discourse, which we have titled *Creation and Redemption*.[3]

                                    *   *   *

---

1. Executive director of Agudas Chasidei Chabad in America during the 1930's, Rabbi Jacobson (1895-1975) was intimately involved in the effort to rescue Rabbi Yosef Yitzchak from war-ravaged Europe in 1940.

2. *Out of the Inferno* (Kehot, 2002), p. 293-4.

3. See *Bati Legani 5711* (*Sefer Hamaamarim Melukat*, vol. 1, p. 5), where this discourse is described as one that Rabbi Yosef Yitzchak delivered "at the beginning of his arrival to America (*bitchilat bo'o le'America*)." See below, footnote 246 to main text.

THE DISCOURSE

Rabbi Yosef Yitzchak examines two general Divine revelations, one that conforms to the natural realm and one that transcends it—*Creation* vs. *Transcendence*. He elaborates primarily upon Creation, which is brought into being through the Divine attribute of *malchut*,[4] kingship.[5] *Malchut* causes limitation, definition and thus revelation. But the limitation of *malchut*—through myriad stages of devolution—can lead ultimately to limitation in an unholy sense, to the imprisonment of the soul and the human being. Transcendence—a revelation of the Essence of the Infinite One— makes liberation and redemption possible.

INTRODUCTIONS

When G-d introduces Himself to the Jewish people at Sinai, He identifies Himself as the one *who brought you out of the land of Egypt.*[6]

Presuming that the purpose of this piece of information is to impress His greatness upon the Israelites, would it not have been more effective for G-d to mention that He is the Creator of the universe? Granted the miracles in Egypt were remarkable, but can they compare to the wonder of creation?[7]

The Rebbe raises this famous question in the second chapter of this discourse. He amplifies the question by contrasting the nature of a miracle with that of creation. A miracle involves an unnatural transformation of something-from-something. Creation, however, means to "bring into being," to create something-from-nothing. To turn a staff into a snake, for example, is to take one existent object, a "something," and turn it into a different "something." This is less

---

4. See below, footnote 68 to main text.

5. The attribute of *malchut*, kingship, corresponds to the Divine faculty of "speech," for a king rules his people primarily through spoken decrees. As the verse states (Ecclesiastes 8:4), *A king's **word** is authoritative....*

6. Exodus 20:2.

7. This question is raised by early Biblical commentators; see below, footnote 24 to main text, where a few of their answers are cited.

remarkable than the creation of heaven and earth, in which
G-d brought matter into being out of absolute nothingness. It
was not a manipulation of one type of entity to another but a
creation of something entirely new. Certainly something-
from-nothing is more remarkable than something-from-
something.[8]

The Rebbe answers the question as follows: At both
Creation and the Exodus, a revelation of Divinity occurred.
However, the revelation that occurred at the Exodus was a
revelation of G-d's *Essence*, while the revelation of Creation
was a revelation of G-d's *radiance*.

G-d therefore does not introduce Himself as the Creator
of heaven and earth, since at Sinai G-d revealed His *Essence*—and calling Himself the Creator does not imply His
Essence.[9]

CREATION

Before the world came into being, finiteness did not exist. In
order for finiteness to emerge from the Infinite, the attribute
of *malchut* was required. *Malchut* is synonymous with the Divine name *Elokim*—the name with which the world was
created (as in the opening verse of Genesis: *In the beginning
Elokim created*)—and represents *tzimtzum*, the contraction

---

8. In a wonderful digression, however, the Rebbe questions his own as-
sertion. He says that although a staff
turning into a snake may appear to be
something-from-something, it is essentially no different than the creation of something-from-nothing—for
since the new entity is of an altogether different substance, nature and
life-force than its predecessor, its existence is therefore just as miraculous
as that of an entirely new being.

Nevertheless, the Rebbe defers unquestioningly to the opinion of his
predecessor, Rabbi Schneur Zalman
of Liadi, who, in his work *Shaar Hay-*

ichud Veha'emunah, deems the manipulation of nature to be less of a
miracle than its creation. And so the
question stands. See below, footnotes
47 and 48 to main text.

9. Creation is effected by a manifestation of G-dly light and radiance—not
by a revelation of His Essence. The
Exodus from Egypt, however, came
about only through a revelation of
G-d's Essence. That is why at Sinai,
when G-d revealed His Essence to the
Children of Israel, He refers to Himself as the G-d *who brought you out of
the land of Egypt*.

and concealment of Divine light. The attribute of *malchut* creates limitation and definition. In the Rebbe's words:[10]

> The creation of the worlds, therefore, required at its root the attribute of *malchut*, kingship. This idea is expressed in the verse, *Your kingship (*malchut*) is a kingship (*malchut*) over all worlds*[11]— i.e., the creation of all worlds stems from the attribute of *malchut*.
>
> The same idea is expressed in the phrase, "You are the only One—the life of [all] the worlds, O King"[12]: to proceed from the Infinite Light, which is One and Unique, to "life of [all] the worlds," requires the attribute of "King"—*malchut*.

But the limitation of *malchut* can lead ultimately to limitation in an unholy sense, to the imprisonment of the soul and the human being. The revelation of G-d's Essence, on the other hand, creates an exodus from the limitations created by *malchut*. On the physical plane, the revelation of Essence causes an exodus from physical limitation, such as from *Mitzraim*. (*Mitzraim* is the Hebrew name for Egypt and means "borders" or "limitations.")

This, in short, takes us through chapters 2-7 of the discourse. However, we have omitted the discourse's elaborate discussion regarding the nature of *malchut* and its distinction from the other attributes. We will now rectify that omission.

ABRAHAM

> *G-d had tampered with the weather. He had removed the sun from its sheath and allowed it to shine with full vigor. Why? So that Abraham would not have to tend to guests. It was the third day following his circumcision, when the pain is greatest, and G-d wished to give Abraham, the perpetual host, a reprieve. Not one traveler passed by Abraham's four-door tent on that day.*

---

10. Ch. 3 of discourse.

11. Psalms 145:13.

12. Liturgy, *Baruch She'amar.*

Well-intentioned as this gesture was, it did not make Abraham happy. He was pained by the fact that he did not have an opportunity to invite guests to his home. He sat at the door of his tent desperately scanning the sands for someone upon whom to bestow his kindness.[13]

This story is cited not to demonstrate the greatness of Abraham—that will come later, at the end of the discourse—but rather to contrast the attribute of *malchut* with that of *chesed*, kindness. As we see from Abraham, the attribute of kindness does not require the presence of a recipient. Abraham's kindness was fully functional and animated despite the absence of any would-be beneficiary. So much so that his inability to actualize his kindness caused him pain.

The same is true of man's other attributes. Like kindness, they can exist without a recipient. The attribute of *malchut*, however, does not function and cannot be animated without the presence of subjects.

COAL AND FLINT

The cause for this distinction is the latent manner in which *malchut* is found prior to its revelation.

There are two manners in which something can be latent. The first can be compared to the latency of fire within a piece of flint and the second to the latency of fire within a hot coal.

The fire contained within the hot coal can be termed a latent fire since it is hidden and invisible on the surface. But this concealment is only visual. The fire actually exists (latent) within the coal; it is just that one cannot see it when looking at the coal.

The latency of the flint's fire, on the other hand, is much more severe. There is no actual fire or heat within the piece of flint. The "fire" exists only in potential form—striking flint against steel produces sparks, which create fire—but not in actuality.

These two manners of latency determine just how easily

---

13. *Bava Metzia* 86b.

the fire will become revealed. Since the latency of the coal's fire is only incidental, it lends itself naturally to revelation. One need only hold a flammable substance in close proximity to the coal and it will burst into flames. Not so with the flint's "fire." Here the latency is part of the nature of the (potential) fire's "existence," by virtue of the fact that there is no actual fire within the flint. As such, it is a latency that does not naturally lend itself to revelation. The fire of the flint can therefore be extracted only with great effort, while the fire in the coal emerges with ease.

A similar distinction can be made between the attribute of *malchut* and the rest of the attributes. All of the attributes exist in latent form prior to their revelation. A person does not acquire the attribute of kindness when he is animated with that emotion; he possesses the attribute prior to its animation, in a latent form. However, this latency is like that of the fire in a piece of coal; it is a latency that lends itself to revelation. Kindness can therefore be easily animated without the actual presence of a recipient, and even by a member of a different species, such as an animal.

The latency of *malchut*, on the other hand, is of a different sort altogether; its latency is not well-disposed to revelation. Its latency is like that of a fire within a flint; therefore, much effort is required for it to be revealed. The feeling of *malchut* (kingship and exaltedness) will not be evoked within a person without the presence of others, and those others must be fellow human beings. The presence of a million animals will not evoke any sense of *malchut* within a human being.

SUPERNAL ATTRIBUTES

The Rebbe now turns to the supernal realms and applies the distinction of *malchut* in humans to the Divine attribute of *malchut*.

Whereas the other Divine attributes are "Self-animated," the attribute of *malchut*—Divine kingship—is animated only by human instigation. The other six Divine attributes were revealed in the Six Days of Creation by G-d's own initiative, while the seventh attribute, *malchut*, was evoked only after Adam, the first human, crowned G-d as King.

The other Divine attributes *influence* creation, but do not exist expressly *for the purpose of* creation.[14] *Malchut*, by contrast, is manifest solely for the sake of creation.

So just as the human attribute of *malchut* is elicited and animated only through others—"There is no king without a nation"[15]—likewise, the supernal attribute of *malchut* is revealed only for the sake of creation.[16]

MALCHUT AND NAME

It is for this reason that the attribute of *malchut*, Divine kingship, is called "name." (The second phrase of the *Adon Olam* prayer reads: "His *name* was proclaimed *King*.")

A name exists only for the sake of others. If you are alone on an island, you do not need a name. A name is necessary

---

14. The Rebbe offers the example of "emotions of the intellect" as an entity that relates to entities beneath it but yet does not exist for the sake of that lower entity.

We generally think of emotions as existing within the heart. The Rebbe introduces us to emotions of the intellect. When a person is excited by an intellectual idea, that excitement is the emotions of intellect.

The emotions of the intellect relate to the emotions of the heart. They are of the same realm and serve as the bridge between intellect and emotions. But one would not say that they exist for the sake of the emotions of the heart. In fact, their existence completes the *intellect*, proving that the person has truly understood what he has studied. "A lack of [intellectual] excitement," says the Rebbe, "is a sign of a lack of understanding."

So the purely intellectual aspect of intellect does not relate at all to emotions and therefore does not serve as the source for emotions. It is the emotional aspect of intellect, the excitement of intellectual experience, that relates to the emotions of the heart and therefore serves as the source for them. However, this does not mean that they exist *for the sake of* the emotions of the heart.

15. See sources cited below, footnote 111 to main text.

16. *Malchut* can thus be seen as the attribute furthest from the Divine Essence, since it comes into being not as a Self-initiated revelation, but as something that is instigated by the lower creatures. This further underscores the inferiority of the Divine revelation that occurred at Creation, which was of *malchut*, and the superiority of the revelation at the Exodus, which was of the Divine Essence.

only so that you can be differentiated from others and identified.

Malchut is therefore called "name," since it exists only in the presence of and for the sake of others.

Now, although "name" symbolizes how an entity relates to other entities, it is also the conduit through which that being receives life. [The name of a human being, for example, is the conduit through which the energy of the soul is channeled to the body.]

This aspect of a name is true of *malchut* as well, since *malchut* is the conduit through which the worlds' life-force is channeled.

MALCHUT OF ATZILUT

Here the discourse qualifies what it had earlier posited about *malchut*: There is a level of *malchut*—Supernal *malchut*—that does differ from the terrestrial sort. Supernal *malchut* can exist without subjects.

As *malchut* exists in *Atzilut*, prior to the creation of worlds, it exists as an "inherent exaltedness"[17] and does not require the presence of subjects over which to lord.

This level of *malchut* is referred to in the phrase with which the *Adon Olam* prayer begins: "Lord of the universe, *who reigned before anything was created.*"

It is only when *malchut* descends into the lower worlds, where it can function as actual kingship, that we say "There is no king without a nation."

REVELATION THROUGH DEFINITION

Nevertheless, even in *Atzilut*, *malchut* is called "name," since *malchut* causes revelation. Even as it exists in *Atzilut*, *malchut*'s function is to limit, define and thereby reveal.

An example: The attribute of kindness as it exists without the element of *malchut* is a vague notion of kindness without any specific direction. It is *malchut* that defines that kindness and "decides" whether it will be a spiritual kindness or

---

17. See below, ch. 6 and footnote 137.

physical kindness, how the kindness is to be delivered, etc. [Without the *malchut* element, the kindness can be completely inappropriate for the recipient. *Malchut* contemplates the capacity and needs of the recipient and conditions the manifestation of the kindness accordingly. Similarly, the Divine attribute of *chochmah*, wisdom, would be entirely meaningless and inaccessible to the creatures if it were not limited and defined by *malchut* of *chochmah*.]

Malchut is therefore said to be the "actuality" (*yeshut u'metziut*) of any given attribute; it reveals and defines all that is nebulous and potential.

But the limitation of *malchut* can ultimately lead to limitation of the "other side"—the impure realm—and result in the imprisonment of the soul, which while clothed in an animal consciousness can lose its spiritual sensitivity and Divine awareness. It is only through the revelation of G-d's Infinite Essence that liberation and redemption can occur. This occurred during the Exodus from Egypt (*Mitzraim*) and at the revelation at Sinai. G-d therefore does not say *I am the L-rd... who created heaven and earth*, since Creation stems from the Divine power of *malchut*, which ultimately leads to limitations and spiritual imprisonment—"*Mitzraim*." At Sinai, when G-d revealed His Essence, He describes Himself specifically as the one who liberated the Israelites from Egypt, since it is only through a revelation of His Essence that liberation occurs.

NISSAN AND TISHREI

These two types of revelations—*malchut* and Essence—are embodied by the two months of Tishrei and Nissan.

The Midrash states[18] that G-d chose two different beginnings of years. One beginning was when He created the world (Tishrei), and another when He chose Jacob and his descendants. The second beginning takes place in Nissan—the month of redemption.

---

18. *Shemot Rabbah* 15:11.

Tishrei represents the revelation of Divinity within the context of nature (*malchut*), whereas Nissan represents redemption, the revelation of Divinity that does not conform to the garments of nature (G-d's Essence).

Hence the seemingly redundant verse with which the discourse begins: *This month is for you the first of months; it is, for you, the first of the months of the year* (Exodus 12:2). There are two types of *months*, i.e., Divine revelations.[19] *Months of the year* refers to a revelation that is limited, represented by Creation and Tishrei. The other type of *months* is plain *months*, unspecified and unlimited. This is the month of Nissan, the month of redemption and unlimited revelation. This revelation occurs only *for you*, i.e., the souls of Israel. Furthermore, even in *the months of the year*—within the context of the world's natural garments—it will be *this month*, i.e., the month of redemption, which transcends nature. In the Rebbe's words, "Divinity that transcends nature will be sensed even within nature."[20]

This essentially concludes the discourse. However, a seemingly separate discussion takes place at the end of the discourse, where the Rebbe leads up to a discussion in which he passionately lauds Abraham's work in teaching the world about G-d and criticizes the insularism of Noah and the other righteous individuals who lived prior to Abraham.

FUTURE REDEMPTION

The Talmud records[21] a difference of opinion as to whether the final redemption will take place in Nissan or Tishrei. What is the logic behind these two opinions?

The Midrash speaks[22] of the seventh as being precious: the seventh day of the week, Shabbat, is precious; the seventh son of Yishai, David, is precious. So if Nissan is the month of redemption, it follows that the seventh month after that is considered to be precious. That accounts for the opinion that the

---

19. See below, ch. 7 and footnote 178.   21. *Rosh Hashanah* 11a.

20. End of discourse.   22. *Vayikra Rabbah* 29:11.

future redemption will take place in Tishrei, which is seven months after Nissan.

To explain the other opinion, the Rebbe offers three explanations. Firstly, Tishrei is a time of judgment and therefore not appropriate for redemption. Secondly, in Tishrei, the Divine beneficence is dependent on and commensurate to human endeavor. In Nissan, however, G-d's blessing upon man transcends his behavior. Nissan is therefore the proper month for redemption—a revelation that completely transcends the natural order.

Thirdly, the preciousness of the seventh does not mean that it is greater than the first. In fact, without the first there can be no seventh.

THE PRECIOUSNESS OF ABRAHAM

The Midrash speaks of the seven Patriarchs, beginning with Abraham and ending with Moses. Yet, although Moses—the seventh—is singled out as precious, his greatness is attributed to the first, Abraham. Thus, when Moses responds to G-d with the same expression used by Abraham (*hineni*—"here I am"[23]), G-d chastises him, saying, *In the place of great ones do not stand!*[24]

The Midrash says[25] that prior to Abraham the world was shrouded in spiritual darkness. With the emergence of Abraham spiritual light began to illuminate the world.

What was so special about Abraham? Were there not righteous men before him—Enoch, Methuselah, Noah?

The Rebbe explains that while these individuals were indeed righteous, the world at large remained dark because their righteousness was self-contained. There deeds therefore had no effect upon the world. Abraham was the first who sought to bring the truth of the One G-d to all mankind. He did not wait for people to come to him and ask him

---

23. Exodus 3:4.

24. Proverbs 25:6. See below, foot-note 227 to main text.

25. *Bereishit Rabbah* 2:3.

about G-d—he went to them. And he did this with self-sacrifice.

ABRAHAM AND R. AKIVA

In what appears to be a tangent,[26] the Rebbe elaborates upon the nature of Abraham's self-sacrifice and how it surpassed that of R. Akiva. R. Akiva waited all his life for the opportunity to give up his life for G-d and was therefore happy when he was being ruthlessly killed by the Romans. This is a self-sacrifice that fulfills the spiritual desire of the individual.

Abraham, on the other hand, did not seek self-sacrifice; he sought to fulfill the will of G-d. If that entailed self-sacrifice—so be it. But he did not seek self-sacrifice. Abraham thus did not enjoy the time he spent in prison,[27] since he was then unable to teach his fellow creatures about G-d.

So Abraham was the first to reveal G-dliness in the world. And Moses, the seventh after Abraham, is precious only because of Abraham's pioneering efforts. Thus, in this respect, the first is greater than the seventh.

Similarly, although Tishrei is the seventh after Nissan, its very preciousness derives from the fact that it is seventh to Nissan, completing what Nissan began—which only demonstrates the greatness of Nissan. Hence the (accepted) opinion that the final redemption will occur in Nissan.

---

26. See *Bati Legani*, ibid.; cited below, footnote 246 to main text.

27. See below, footnote 245 to main text.

EDITORIAL NOTES

In vocalizing the Hebrew words in this edition we have followed the grammatical rules of the Holy Tongue, which occasionally differ from the traditional or colloquial pronunciation.

The footnotes that appear in the original Hebrew edition of the discourse have been translated and appear here in bold type. All other footnotes are the work of the translator. The translator has also added comments to the original footnotes.

Regarding the footnotes that appear in the original Hebrew edition, see the introduction written by the Lubavitcher Rebbe, Rabbi Menachem M. Schneerson (son-in-law and successor of the author) to the first edition of *Sefer Hamaamarim Kayitz 5700*, dated 12 Menachem Av 5711 (1951): "...references to verses and to statements of our Sages of blessed memory from Talmud and Midrash are the work of Rabbi Dovber Ushpal.... The references to statements of the *Zohar*, writings of the Arizal, Chasidic works and short comments are the work of the publisher." The publisher is the Lubavitcher Rebbe himself.

In the first appendix, the footnotes appearing in bold type are a translation of the Lubavitcher Rebbe's notes to the original Yiddish edition of *Lessons in Tanya* (*Shiurim Besefer Hatanya*, Kehot, 1984).

TRANSLATION
AND
COMMENTARY

With the Assistance of Heaven,

Shabbat Parshat Tazria, Parshat Hachodesh,[1] *5700 (1940)*

This month is for you the first of months; it is, for you, the first of the months of the year.[2]

The second half of the verse—*it is, for you, the first of the months of the year*—seems to be a restatement of the first half: *this month is for you the first of months.* Why does the Torah repeat itself? Additionally, why is the verse so verbose—*it is, for you, the first of the months of the year?* It would have been sufficient had the verse just said, *it is the first of the months of the year.*

From all of this it is understood that there are two dynamics here: 1) *Firsts of months*; and 2) *months of the year.* And although *this month is for you the first of months*, nevertheless, *it is, for you, the first of the months of the year.* In other words, both dynamics are necessary: *firsts of months*, and *months of the year* [as we shall explain].[3]

DUAL BEGINNINGS

The explanation is as follows. *Midrash Rabbah*[4] states:

> When G-d chose His world,[5] He established in it firsts of months and years. And when He chose Jacob and his sons, He established in it a first month of redemption.

This, then, is [the explanation of our verse] *This month is for you the first of months; it is, for you, the first of the months of the year.*

---

1. *Parshat Hachodesh* (Exodus 12:1-20) is read as a supplemental Torah portion on the Shabbat that precedes the first day of Nissan (or on the first day of Nissan if it occurs on Shabbat). It discusses the commandment from G-d, given on Rosh Chodesh Nissan, concerning the Paschal sacrifice.

2. **Exodus 12:2.** This verse refers to

the month of Nissan.

3. In short, the Rebbe's answer will be that *months of the year* refers to Divine revelation that permeates the natural realm, while *first of months* refers to Divine revelation that remains transcendent from nature. The verse is saying that *for you*, i.e., the Jewish people, the supernatural will be ex-

בס״ד, ש״פ תזריע, פרשת החודש, ש״ת.

הַחֹדֶשׁ הַזֶּה[א] לָכֶם רֹאשׁ חֳדָשִׁים, רִאשׁוֹן הוּא לָכֶם לְחָדְשֵׁי הַשָּׁנָה.

וְצָרִיךְ לְהָבִין, מַדּוּעַ כּוֹפֵל הָעִנְיָן בְּאוֹמְרוֹ רִאשׁוֹן הוּא לָכֶם לְחָדְשֵׁי הַשָּׁנָה, שֶׁהֲרֵי כְּבָר נֶאֱמַר הַחֹדֶשׁ הַזֶּה לָכֶם רֹאשׁ חֳדָשִׁים, וְלָמָּה כּוֹפֵל — וּבַאֲרִיכוּת כָּזוֹ — רִאשׁוֹן הוּא לָכֶם לְחָדְשֵׁי הַשָּׁנָה. דְּבְכָל אֹפֶן הָיָה מַסְפִּיק שֶׁיֹּאמַר רִאשׁוֹן לְחָדְשֵׁי הַשָּׁנָה.

דְּמִכְּלָלוּת הָעִנְיָן מוּבָן שֶׁיֵּשׁ ב׳ בְּחִינוֹת: הָא׳ רָאשֵׁי חֳדָשִׁים, וְהַב׳ חָדְשֵׁי הַשָּׁנָה, וְעִם הֱיוֹת דְּהַחֹדֶשׁ הַזֶּה לָכֶם רֹאשׁ חֳדָשִׁים מִכָּל מָקוֹם רִאשׁוֹן הוּא לָכֶם לְחָדְשֵׁי הַשָּׁנָה, הַיְינוּ שֶׁצָּרִיךְ לִהְיוֹת שְׁתֵּי הַמַּדְרֵיגוֹת, רָאשֵׁי חֳדָשִׁים וְחָדְשֵׁי הַשָּׁנָה.

אַךְ הָעִנְיָן הוּא, דְּאִיתָא בְּמִדְרָשׁ רַבָּה:

מִשֶּׁבָּחַר הַקָּדוֹשׁ בָּרוּךְ הוּא[ד] בְּעוֹלָמוֹ קָבַע בּוֹ רָאשֵׁי חֳדָשִׁים וְשָׁנִים, וּמִשֶּׁבָּחַר בְּיַעֲקֹב וּבָנָיו קָבַע בּוֹ רֹאשׁ חֹדֶשׁ שֶׁל גְּאוּלָה.

וְזֶהוּ הַחֹדֶשׁ הַזֶּה לָכֶם רֹאשׁ חֳדָשִׁים, רִאשׁוֹן הוּא לָכֶם לְחָדְשֵׁי הַשָּׁנָה:

---

perienced even within the natural.

4. *Shemot Rabbah* 15:11.

5. The expression "G-d *chose* His world" alludes to the following account in *Bereshit Rabbah* 9:2: "G-d was creating worlds and destroying them, creating worlds and destroying them. It was only when He created this world that He said: 'This world pleases Me;

the others did not please Me.'"

He then "celebrated" by decorating the heavens with lights—the sun and the moon (just as human beings celebrate by decorating with torches and lanterns). Thus: "When G-d *chose* His world"—over the previous ones that He destroyed—"He established in it firsts of months and years," i.e., the sun and the moon by which years and months are set (*Maharzu* ad loc.).

Months of the year refers to when G-d chose His world. *This month is for you the first of months* refers to when G-d chose Jacob and his sons and established for them a month of redemption, the month of Nissan.[6]

This, however, needs to be understood, for our Sages said, "On Rosh Hashanah slave labor ceased from our forefathers,"[7] which seems to imply that the beginning of the redemption in Egypt took place on Rosh Hashanah.[8] Why, then, is it Nissan that is referred to as the month G-d established—when He chose Jacob and his sons—as the month of redemption?[9]

NISSAN AND TISHREI

Nissan and Tishrei are referred to in the Torah as *first* and *seventh*. Nissan is called *first* and Tishrei *seventh*.[10] The redemption from Egypt, which was the first redemption, took place in Nissan.

However, with regard to the last redemption—which will commence with the coming of Moshiach speedily in our days, Amen—the Talmud[11] records a dispute between R. Eliezer and R. Yehoshua. R. Eliezer maintains that "our forefathers were redeemed in Nissan, and in the future we will be re-

---

6. NISSAN: MONTH OF REDEMPTION. The Midrash continues: "In that month (Nissan), Israel was redeemed from Egypt, and in that month they are destined to be redeemed (in the Messianic era), as it says, *As the days of your leaving Egypt I will show you wonders* (Micah 7:15).

"And in that month Isaac was born [the angels visited Abraham on Pesach and Isaac was born a year later—*Maharzu*] and Isaac was tied as a sacrifice [the Midrash presumes that he 'died' on the same day as he was born, since such is the way of the righteous—*Maharzu*; however, other sources indicate that the binding of Isaac took place in Tishrei, on Yom Kippur—see *Radal* and *Rashash*]. And

it was in that month that Jacob received the blessings [Pesach is the time for the dew prayer and Jacob was indeed blessed with the dew of heaven—*Maharzu*].

"And in that month G-d hinted to Israel that it is a beginning for them in matters of salvation [for all generations—*Maharzu*], as it says, *it is the first of months of the year for you*. This can be compared to a king who removes his son from prison and says, 'Make this day a festival forever, since it is the day that my son emerged from darkness to light, from the iron yoke to life, from slavery to freedom, from subjugation to redemption.' Likewise, [in Nissan] G-d removed Israel from prison...."

דְּחָדְשֵׁי הַשָּׁנָה הוּא מְשֻׁבָּחַר הַקָּדוֹשׁ בָּרוּךְ הוּא בְּעוֹלָמוֹ,
וְהַחֹדֶשׁ הַזֶּה לָכֶם רֹאשׁ חֳדָשִׁים הוּא מְשֻׁבָּחַר בְּיַעֲקֹב וּבָנָיו
קָבַע לָהֶם חֹדֶשׁ שֶׁל גְּאוּלָה, שֶׁהוּא חֹדֶשׁ נִיסָן.

וְצָרִיךְ לְהָבִין, וַהֲלֹא אָמְרוּ רַבּוֹתֵינוּ זִכְרוֹנָם לִבְרָכָה,
בְּרֹאשׁ הַשָּׁנָה בָּטְלָהּ עֲבוֹדָה מֵאֲבוֹתֵינוּ, שֶׁתְּחִלַּת הַגְּאוּלָה
דְּגְאוּלַת מִצְרַיִם הָיְתָה בְּרֹאשׁ הַשָּׁנָה, וְלָמָּה זֶה מַה
שֶּׁבָּחַר הַקָּדוֹשׁ בָּרוּךְ הוּא בְּיַעֲקֹב וּבָנָיו קָבַע לָהֶם חֹדֶשׁ שֶׁל
גְּאוּלָה, הוּא נִיסָן.

וְהִנֵּה נִיסָן וְתִשְׁרֵי נִקְרָאִים בַּתּוֹרָה רִאשׁוֹן וּשְׁבִיעִי, דְּנִיסָן
נִקְרָא רִאשׁוֹן וְתִשְׁרֵי שְׁבִיעִי. וּגְאוּלַת מִצְרַיִם שֶׁהִיא גְּאוּלָה
רִאשׁוֹנָה הָיְתָה בְּנִיסָן.

וְהִנֵּה בִּזְמַן הַגְּאוּלָה דְּגָלוּת הָאַחֲרוֹן, בְּבִיאַת הַמָּשִׁיחַ
בִּמְהֵרָה בְיָמֵינוּ אָמֵן, יֵשׁ פְּלוּגְתָּא בִּגְמָרָא⁷, רַבִּי אֱלִיעֶזֶר וְרַבִּי
יְהוֹשֻׁעַ, דְּרַבִּי אֱלִיעֶזֶר סְבִירָא לֵיהּ דִּבְנִיסָן נִגְאֲלוּ אֲבוֹתֵינוּ

Shemot Rabbah 18:11-2 offers other examples of redemptions that took place in Nissan, on the night of Pesach, which is referred to in Scripture (Exodus 12:42) as the *night of guardings* [plural, alluding to the many cases of *guardings* that would take place on that night throughout history—*Yefei Toar*]: Joseph's release from prison [see, however, *Rosh Hashanah* 11a, where it is agreed upon by R. Eliezer and R. Yehoshua that Joseph left prison on Rosh Hashanah —*Radal*]; Hezekiah's salvation; the salvation of Hananiah, Mishael and Azariah; Daniel's salvation from the lion's den; and the emergence of Moshiach and Elijah.

7. *Rosh Hashanah* **11a.**

8. The first of Tishrei.

9. I.e., since it was in Tishrei that our forefathers were freed from their slave labor in Egypt, why is Tishrei not referred to as the month of redemption?

10. Nissan is referred to as the *first month* in Exodus 12:2, Leviticus 23:5 and Numbers 28:16. Tishrei is referred to as the *seventh month* in Leviticus 23:24, 27, 34 and Numbers 29:1, 7, 12.

11. *Rosh Hashanah* **ibid.**

deemed in Tishrei." R. Yehoshua maintains that "our fore-fathers were redeemed in Nissan, and in the future we will be redeemed in Nissan."

This requires clarification: What exactly is at the root of their argument regarding the time of the future re-demption—which will take place speedily in our days, Amen—whether it will be in Nissan or Tishrei? In addition, [why is it that] the *Midrash Rabbah*[12] sides with[13] the view of R. Yehoshua that "our forefathers were redeemed in Nissan, and in the future we will be redeemed in Nissan"?

THEN AND NOW

[In connection with the dedication of the first Temple] the verse states: *All Israel assembled before King Solomon in the month of eitanim, which is the seventh month, for the holiday [of Sukkot].*[14]

Targum Yonatan[15] interprets the verse as follows: *[All Israel assembled before King Solomon] in the month that the ancient ones*[16] *used to call the first month, and which is now the seventh month, for the holiday [of Sukkot].* In other words, "ancient ones," prior to the giving of the Torah, called Tishrei the first month.

For [as the Midrash says] the world was created on the 25th of Elul.[17] The month of Tishrei is therefore the first month for years, as it says, *And they [the heavenly hosts] shall be as signs and testaments, for days and for years.*[18] And the first of Tishrei is Rosh Hashanah.

---

12. **Ibid.**

13. *Hichriu vesatam* in the Hebrew; lit., "decided and stated plainly" [without citing a particular Sage]. In other words, the Midrash makes no mention of there being two opinions as to when the future redemption will take place; it just states plainly (as if it is a given) that it will occur in the month of Nissan.

14. I Kings 8:2.

15. Ad loc.

16. I.e., the people who lived in the era before the giving of the Torah, as the Rebbe now explains. (*Eitan* means "old" or "ancient." This is the basis of *Targum Yonatan's* interpretation.)

17. *Vayikra Rabbah* beginning of

וּבְתִשְׁרֵי עֲתִידִין לְהִגָּאֵל, וְרַבִּי יְהוֹשֻׁעַ סְבִירָא לֵיהּ דִּבְנִיסָן נִגְאֲלוּ אֲבוֹתֵינוּ וּבְנִיסָן עֲתִידִין לְהִגָּאֵל.

וְצָרִיךְ לְהָבִין שֹׁרֶשׁ עִנְיַן מַחֲלוּקְתָּם בִּזְמַן הַגְּאוּלָה הָעֲתִידָה בְּבִיאַת הַמָּשִׁיחַ בִּמְהֵרָה בְּיָמֵינוּ אָמֵן, אִם בְּנִיסָן אוֹ בְּתִשְׁרֵי. וּבְמִדְרָשׁ רַבָּה הִכְרִיעוֹ[י] וְסָתַם כִּדְעַת רַבִּי יְהוֹשֻׁעַ דִּבְנִיסָן, דִּבְנִיסָן נִגְאֲלוּ אֲבוֹתֵינוּ מִמִּצְרַיִם וּבְנִיסָן עֲתִידִין לְהִגָּאֵל.

וְהִנֵּה כְּתִיב וַיִּקָּהֲלוּ[י] אֶל הַמֶּלֶךְ שְׁלֹמֹה כָּל אִישׁ יִשְׂרָאֵל בְּיֶרַח הָאֵיתָנִים בְּחַג הוּא הַחֹדֶשׁ הַשְּׁבִיעִי.

וְתִרְגֵּם בְּיוֹנָתָן בְּיַרְחָא דְּעַתִּיקַיָּא דְּקָרְן לֵיהּ יַרְחָא קַדְמָאָה בְּחַגָּא וּכְעַן הוּא יַרְחָא שְׁבִיעָאָה, עַתִּיקַיָּא קוֹדֶם מַתַּן תּוֹרָה הֲווֹ קָרִין לֵיהּ יַרְחָא קַדְמָאָה.

דְּהִנֵּה בְּכ"ה בֶּאֱלוּל נִבְרָא הָעוֹלָם[י], וְחֹדֶשׁ תִּשְׁרֵי הוּא רֹאשׁ לַשָּׁנִים, כְּמוֹ שֶׁכָּתוּב וְהָיוּ לְאוֹתוֹת[י] וּלְמוֹעֲדִים וּלְיָמִים וְשָׁנִים, וְרִאשׁוֹן בְּתִשְׁרֵי הוּא רֹאשׁ הַשָּׁנָה.

---

sec. 29; *Pesikta, Bachodesh Hashvi'i.* The *Baraita* that says that the world was created in Tishrei refers to the *completion* of the creation (*Ran, Rosh Hashanah* 16a)—i.e., Adam, who was created on the sixth day of Creation, the 1st of Tishrei, and who is considered to have "completed" the entire work of Creation.

18. **Genesis 1:14. How this verse proves the point requires some further study.**

This verse teaches that G-d created different segments in time: *days* and *years.* Now, just as a day has a beginning and an end, so too a year has a beginning and an end. Considering that (according to R. Eliezer) the beginning of Creation was on the 25th of Elul, and that Adam—the "crown" of Creation—was created on the 1st of Tishrei, it follows then that Tishrei is "the first month for [the counting of] years."

Our Sages thus said:

> In accordance with which view do we now pray [on Rosh Hashanah with the words], "This is the day, the beginning of Your creation, a remembrance of the first day"[19]?

—In other words, Rosh Hashanah, which takes place on the first of Tishrei, is "the beginning of Your creation" each year, since it is "a remembrance of the first day" that Creation was completed with the creation of Adam.—

> In accordance with which view [was this prayer composed]? With the view of R. Eliezer, who maintains that the world was created on the 25th of Elul.[20]

"And which is now the seventh month": After the Exodus and the giving of the Torah, Tishrei is the seventh month, as Nissan is the first month.

But if Tishrei was originally called the first, what changed that caused Nissan to be called the first? And if the cause is the redemption that took place in Nissan[21]—that itself requires explanation: *Why* did the redemption take place in Nissan? The beginning of the redemption took place in Tishrei, as it was on Rosh Hashanah—which is in Tishrei—that slave labor ceased from our forefathers. So why did the complete redemption take place in Nissan?[22]

---

19. Liturgy, Musaf for Rosh Hashanah.

20. See *Rosh Hashanah* 27a; *Vayikra Rabbah* and *Pesikta* ibid.

There is a Talmudic debate as to when the world was created. R. Eliezer maintains that Creation commenced on the 25th of Elul, while R. Yehoshua maintains that Creation commenced on the 25th of Adar. Therefore, the prayer of Rosh Hashanah (the 1st of Tishrei) that proclaims "This is the day, the beginning of Your creation..." obviously follows the opinion of R. Eliezer, and not R. Yehoshua.

דְּזֶהוּ שֶׁאָמְרוּ רַבּוֹתֵינוּ זִכְרוֹנָם לִבְרָכָה:

כְּמַאן מְצַלִּינָן הָאִידָנָא זֶה הַיּוֹם תְּחִלַּת מַעֲשֶׂיךָ זִכָּרוֹן
לְיוֹם רִאשׁוֹן

— דְּרֹאשׁ הַשָּׁנָה, שֶׁהוּא בְּיוֹם א׳ דְּתִשְׁרֵי, הוּא תְּחִלַּת
מַעֲשֶׂיךָ בְּכָל שָׁנָה וְשָׁנָה לִהְיוֹתוֹ זִכָּרוֹן לְיוֹם רִאשׁוֹן שֶׁנִּגְמְרָה
הַיְצִירָה וְנִבְרָא אָדָם הָרִאשׁוֹן —

כְּמַאן, כְּרַבִּי אֱלִיעֶזֶר, דִּסְבִירָא לֵיהּ דִּבְכֵּ״ה בְּאֱלוּל נִבְרָא
הָעוֹלָם.

וּכְעַן הוּא יַרְחָא שְׁבִיעָאָה, דְּאַחַר יְצִיאַת מִצְרַיִם וּמַתַּן
תּוֹרָה הִנֵּה חֹדֶשׁ תִּשְׁרֵי הוּא חֹדֶשׁ הַשְּׁבִיעִי, דְּחֹדֶשׁ נִיסָן הוּא
חֹדֶשׁ הָרִאשׁוֹן.

וְצָרִיךְ לְהָבִין, דְּמֵאַחַר דְּמִתְּחִלָּה תִּשְׁרֵי נִקְרָא רִאשׁוֹן, לָמָה
נִשְׁתַּנָּה שֶׁנִּיסָן נִקְרָא רִאשׁוֹן, וְאִם מִפְּנֵי הַגְּאוּלָה שֶׁהָיְתָה
בְּנִיסָן, הָא גוּפָא קַשְׁיָא, לָמָה הָיְתָה הַגְּאוּלָה בְּנִיסָן, שֶׁהֲרֵי
אַתְחַלְתָּא דִגְאוּלָּה הָיָה בְּתִשְׁרֵי, דְּבְרֹאשׁ הַשָּׁנָה שֶׁהוּא בְּתִשְׁרֵי
בָּטְלָה עֲבוֹדָה מֵאֲבוֹתֵינוּ, הִנֵּה לָמָה הַגְּאוּלָה שְׁלֵמָה הָיְתָה
בְּנִיסָן דַּוְקָא.

---

21. I.e., the Exodus from Egypt, which occurred on the 15th of Nissan.

22. Since the "beginning" of the Exodus occurred in Tishrei (the first month of the year) with the ceasing of slave labor, it would seem that there is some connection between the concept of redemption and the month of Tishrei. Why, then, did the complete Exodus occur in Nissan—which subsequently causes Nissan to become the first month?

The Rebbe does not directly answer this question in this discourse. See, however, below, footnote 192.

2.

The explanation of the matter is as follows. It is written, *I am the L-rd your G-d who brought you out of the land of Egypt.*[23]

This needs to be understood: Why does G-d mention the Exodus from Egypt and not the creation of heaven and earth, which was a much greater miracle than the Exodus?[24]

The miracles that occurred with the Exodus from Egypt involved the manipulation of something-from-something,[25] e.g., the staff that turned into a snake[26] and the water that turned to blood[27]—and likewise at the splitting of the sea, where the water stood erect like a wall.[28] All these miracles were the manipulation of something-from-something.

But the creation of heaven and earth is a creation of something-from-nothing.[29] It would therefore seem that G-d should have said, *[I am the L-rd...]* **who created heaven and earth.**[30]

THE NATURE OF A MIRACLE

The truth is[31] that when we apply the expression something-from-something to the miracles of the Exodus, we mean that the something turned into another something, one with a different nature.

This is certainly so in the case of the staff that turned into a snake. In this case, the staff did not just turn into a different entity; it turned into a completely different *category* [of being].[32] At first it was either mineral or vegetable—depending

---

23. **Exodus 20:2.**

24. The Rebbe is not the first to ask this question. Early Biblical commentators address the issue and offer a number of solutions. *Kuzari* (I:25) maintains that G-d speaks of the Exodus since it was something the Israelites had seen with their own eyes, and would therefore mean more to them. *Ibn Ezra* (on verse; see also *Ra-*

shi) argues that G-d refers to His role in the Exodus not to impress the Israelites with His power, but to establish grounds for His imposing special responsibilities upon them, since He had afforded them special treatment in freeing them from Egyptian slavery. See other Biblical commentators on verse.

25. *Yesh me'yesh*, in the Hebrew. I.e.,

ב.

אַךְ הָעִנְיָן הוּא, דְּהִנֵּה כְּתִיב אָנֹכִי ה' אֱלֹקֶיךָ אֲשֶׁר הוֹצֵאתִיךָ מֵאֶרֶץ מִצְרָיִם.

וְצָרִיךְ לְהָבִין, מִפְּנֵי מָה מַזְכִּיר יְצִיאַת מִצְרַיִם וְאֵינוֹ מַזְכִּיר בְּרִיאַת שָׁמַיִם וָאָרֶץ, שֶׁהוּא פֶּלֶא יוֹתֵר גָּדוֹל מִכְּמוֹ יְצִיאַת מִצְרַיִם.

שֶׁהָאוֹתוֹת וּמוֹפְתִים דִּיצִיאַת מִצְרַיִם הֵם יֵשׁ מִיֵּשׁ, וּכְמוֹ הַמַּטֶּה שֶׁנֶּהְפַּךְ לְנָחָשׁ וְהַמַּיִם לְדָם, וְכֵן בִּקְרִיעַת יַם סוּף שֶׁהַמַּיִם נִצְּבוּ כְּמוֹ נֵד, הֲרֵי כָּל זֶה הוּא יֵשׁ מִיֵּשׁ.

אֲבָל בְּרִיאַת שָׁמַיִם וָאָרֶץ הוּא יֵשׁ מֵאַיִן, וַהֲוָה לֵיהּ לְמֵימַר אֲשֶׁר בָּרָאתִי שָׁמַיִם וָאָרֶץ.

וַהֲגַם דְּיֵשׁ מִיֵּשׁ בְּאוֹתוֹת וּמוֹפְתִים דִּיצִיאַת מִצְרַיִם הוּא שֶׁהַיֵּשׁ נֶהְפַּךְ לְיֵשׁ אַחֵר וּבְטֶבַע אַחֶרֶת;

לֹא מִיבָּעֵי בָּזֶה שֶׁהַמַּטֶּה נֶהְפַּךְ לְנָחָשׁ, דְּאֵין זֶה רַק מַה שֶּׁיֵּשׁ זֶה נֶהְפַּךְ לְיֵשׁ אַחֵר, אֶלָּא שֶׁהוּא בְּסוּג אַחֵר לְגַמְרֵי, דִּתְחִלָּה הָיָה דּוֹמֵם אוֹ צוֹמֵחַ, שֶׁיֵּשׁ ב' דֵּעוֹת בַּמַּטֶּה אִם הָיָה

---

these miracles involved the transformation of one form of matter (a "something") into another form of matter (a different "something").

26. Exodus 4:3, 7:10.

27. Ibid. 7:20.

28. Ibid. 14:22, 29.

29. *Yesh me'ayin*, in the Hebrew. I.e., creation *ex nihilo*.

30. If G-d was trying to impress His greatness upon the Children of Israel, he should have mentioned His greatest feat: creation of heaven and earth.

31. The discourse now makes the case that there are two types of something-from-something, one of which is essentially the same as something-from-nothing. As we shall soon see, the miracles of the Exodus were of that type.

32. Generally speaking, physical matter is divided into four primary cat-

on the two opinions regarding the staff, whether it was made of stone[33] or wood[34]—and when it turned into a snake, it entered an entirely different category, that of an animal, and acquired a different nature, that of its new category.

The above is true even in the case of the water that turned to blood. Although the transformation took place within the same category [of being],[35] nevertheless, water and blood are two opposite types of beings, with opposite natures. Water symbolizes *chesed*, kindness, while blood symbolizes *gevurah*, severity.[36] They are also opposite in function.[37]

And it is true even in the case of the splitting of the sea, where the water stood like a wall. Although the *substance* of the water did not change, as the water merely stood like a wall—unlike the water that turned to blood, where the actual *substance* of the water changed and its substance became blood—its *nature* changed. The nature of the water was literally transformed to an opposite nature.[38]

These changes involved not only the substances of these

---

egories, or kingdoms: mineral (*domem*), vegetable (*tzomeach*), animal (*chai*) and human (*medaber*). The miracle of the staff turning into a snake involved not only the transformation of one *entity* into another, but the transformation of an entity from one *category of being* into an entity from another *category of being*.

33. *Shemot Rabbah*, end of *parsha* 8. *Mechilta*, *Shemot*, 17:6.
 Shemot Rabbah ibid.: "Moses said to G-d: 'How am I to bring upon [Pharaoh] ten plagues?' G-d responded, 'You shall take this staff with you.' R. Yehudah said: 'The staff weighed forty *se'ah* and was made of *sapphire*; and the ten plagues were engraved upon it in acronym form: *detzach adash be'achav*.'"
 Mechilta ibid.: "*And you shall hit in*

the rock (Exodus 17:6). The staff of Moses was made of *sapphire*. [For] it does not say *and you shall hit upon the rock*, but rather *and you shall hit in the rock*." This teaches that the staff was made of something very strong that would split the rock (*Rashi* on verse.)

34. *Bamidbar Rabbah*, end of *parsha* 18; *Zohar* II:115a; *Yalkut Reuveni*, *parshat Va'era*; see also *Pirkei d'Rabbi Eliezer* 40.
 The Midrash (ibid.) seeks to identify the staff of Aaron, which sprouted almonds during Korah's revolt (Numbers 17:23). The Midrash cites one opinion that this was the staff of Moses.

35. Both water and blood are inanimate, and are classified within the mineral kingdom.

אֶבֶן* אוֹ עֵץ*, וּכְשֶׁנֶּהְפַּךְ לְנָחָשׁ הֲרֵי נַעֲשָׂה סוּג אַחֵר לְגַמְרֵי שֶׁהוּא חַי, וּבְטֶבַע אַחֶרֶת לְפִי עִנְיַן הַסּוּג;

אֶלָּא שֶׁגַּם בָּזֶה דְּהַמַּיִם נֶהְפְּכוּ לְדָם, הֲגַם שֶׁהוּא בְּאוֹתוֹ הַסּוּג, אֲבָל הֵם מִינֵי יֵשׁ הֲפָכִים זֶה מִזֶּה, הַיְנוּ בִּטְבָעִים הֲפָכִים, דְּמַיִם הֵם חֶסֶד וְדָם גְּבוּרָה, וְהֵם הֲפָכִים בְּעִנְיַן פְּעוּלָּתָם;

אֶלָּא אַף גַּם מַה שֶׁבִּקְרִיעַת יַם סוּף נִצְבוּ כְמוֹ נֵד, עִם הֱיוֹת שֶׁעֶצֶם גּוּף הַמַּיִם לֹא נִשְׁתַּנָּה, דְּאֵינוּ דוֹמֶה לְזֶה שֶׁהַמַּיִם נֶהְפְּכוּ לְדָם, הֲרֵי שֶׁעֶצֶם הַיֵּשׁ דְּמַיִם נִשְׁתַּנָּה לְיֵשׁ דְּדָם, וְכַאֲשֶׁר הַמַּיִם נִצְבוּ כְמוֹ נֵד הִנֵּה עֶצֶם הַיֵּשׁ לֹא נִשְׁתַּנָּה, אֲבָל טִבְעוֹ נִשְׁתַּנָּה, וְהַשִׁנּוּי הוּא בְּטֶבַע הֲפָכִית מַמָּשׁ;

הִנֵּה הַשִׁנּוּיִּים הָאֵלּוּ הֲרֵי אֵין זֶה שֶׁהוּא רַק בְּהַיֵּשׁ שֶׁנֶּהְפַּךְ

---

36. WATER AND CHESED. The nature of water is to descend to a low area; the lower the area, the larger the quantity of water that will gather there. Kindness, too, is expressed only upon a "low" individual; i.e., upon one who is in need of kindness and mercy. One who is imprisoned, for example, will awaken the kindness and mercy of others to the point that they will bring him food there. Likewise, Supernal kindness is elicited by one who is distressed by finding himself "imprisoned" in his body and animal soul, and yearns for G-d (*Likkutei Torah, Derushim l'Rosh Hashanah,* 61c).

BLOOD AND GEVURAH: Anger—a derivative of *gevurah*—is defined as the "boiling of the blood." Now, Scripture states (Deuteronomy 12:23), *The blood is the soul*—i.e., one's pri-

mary energy is from one's soul. When one is disturbed about a given subject matter, he becomes angry. The more the subject matter pertains to one's essence, the angrier he will become. This is because there is more "blood" (i.e., more energy) invested in this subject matter, as it is dearer to him (*Or Hatorah, Derushim l'Yom Kippur,* p. 2134).

37. In humans, for example, water generally cools a person, whereas blood transfers heat to the skin.

38. The fact that water—a free-flowing, moving substance—stood erect and rigid like a wall, demonstrates a complete transformation of the water's nature, from one extreme to the other.

beings, which changed from one substance to another and from one nature to another; the change involved the Divine energy that creates the being.[39] As in the saying, "He who tells oil to burn will tell vinegar to burn."[40]

OIL AND VINEGAR

Our Sages say, "The world was created with ten [Divine] utterances."[41] Every single created being is represented by its specific letters in the "ten utterances," and it is those letters that create and give life to that being.

These letters are the formations of the names of the beings as they are found in the "ten utterances." There are, however, many and varied ways in which these letters are represented. The names of some beings are mentioned explicitly, such as *light, firmament* and other beings. Others are repre-

---

39. Every entity is created and defined by a Divine energy unique to it—a one-of-a-kind, spiritual DNA, so to speak. Therefore, in order for any being to "change" its substance or nature, there must first be a change in the Divine energy that sustains that being, as the discourse will soon explain.

40. *Taanit* 25a (following the version of *Ein Yaakov*).

The Talmud relates: One Friday, R. Chanina ben Dosa, a man well-versed in miracles, noticed that his daughter looked upset. When he asked her what was the matter, she said that she had mistakenly used vinegar to light the Shabbat lamps instead of oil, and the flames would soon burn out. R. Chanina told her not to worry: "He who tells oil to burn will tell vinegar to burn." In the end, the flames burned throughout the entire Shabbat, and were also used for the *Havdalah* flame.

41. *Avot* 5:1.

TEN UTTERANCES. Scripture (Genesis 1) describes the process of Creation as occurring through G-d's "speech": *G-d said, "Let there be light," and there was light... G-d said, "Let there be a firmament in the midst of the waters...," and it was so....* The "ten utterances" refers to the nine times Scripture employs the phrase *G-d said, "Let..."* in its account of Creation, plus the first verse of Genesis, *Bereishit....*, which is also considered to be one of G-d's "utterances" (see *Rosh Hashanah* 32a).

According to Kabbalah and Chasidus, the "ten utterances" are actually the life-force that sustains all of creation. Rabbi Schneur Zalman of Liadi discusses this in *Tanya*, ch. 21: "In the case of the Holy One, blessed be He, His speech is not, heaven forfend, separated from His blessed Self, for there is nothing outside of Him, and there is no place devoid of Him. Therefore, His blessed speech is not like our speech, G-d forbid... His

מִיֵּשׁ לְיֵשׁ וּמִטֶּבַע לְטֶבַע אַחֶרֶת, אֶלָּא שֶׁהֲשִׁינּוּי הוּא בְּהַכֹּחַ הָאֱלֹקִי הַמְהַוֶּוה אֶת הַיֵּשׁ, וּכְמַאֲמָר מִי שֶׁאָמַר לְשֶׁמֶן יֹּ וְיַדְלִיק יֹאמַר לְחוֹמֶץ וְיַדְלִיק.

דְּהִנֵּה אָמְרוּ רַבּוֹתֵינוּ זִכְרוֹנָם לִבְרָכָה, בַּעֲשָׂרָה מַאֲמָרוֹת יֹּ נִבְרָא הָעוֹלָם, דְּכָל נִבְרָא וְנִבְרָא יֵשׁ לוֹ אוֹתִיּוֹת פְּרָטִיוֹת בַּעֲשָׂרָה מַאֲמָרוֹת אֲשֶׁר הָאוֹתִיּוֹת הָהֵם הֵם מְהַוִּוים וּמְחַיִּים אֶת הַנִּבְרָא הַהוּא.

וּבְעִנְיַן הָאוֹתִיּוֹת שֶׁל הַנִּבְרָאִים, שֶׁהֵם צִירוּפֵי שְׁמוֹתֵיהֶם כְּמוֹ שֶׁהֵם בַּעֲשָׂרָה מַאֲמָרוֹת, הֲרֵי יֵשׁ בָּזֶה כַּמָּה בְּחִינוֹת וּמַדְרֵיגוֹת בְּאוֹפַנִּים מֵאוֹפַנִּים שׁוֹנִים, יֵשׁ שֶׁצֵּירוּפֵי שְׁמוֹתֵיהֶם נִזְכְּרוּ מְפוֹרָשׁ בַּעֲשָׂרָה מַאֲמָרוֹת, כְּמוֹ אוֹר וְרָקִיעַ וּשְׁאָרֵי

---

blessed speech is called 'speech' only by way of an anthropomorphic illustration, in the sense that, as in the case of man below, whose speech reveals to his audience what was hidden and concealed in his thoughts, so, too, it is with the blessed *Ein Sof*, whose emitted light and life-force—as it emerges from Him, from concealment into revelation, to create worlds and to sustain them—is called 'speech.' These emanations are, indeed, the 'ten utterances' by which the world was created."

Other creations, not enumerated in the "ten utterances," are created from G-d's speech "by means of numerous and various contractions until the created beings can receive their life and existence from it" (ibid).

In *Shaar Hayichud Veha'emunah* (ch. 1), Rabbi Schneur Zalman expounds on this subject: "It is written (Psalms 119:89): *Forever, O G-d, Your word stands in the heavens.* The Baal Shem Tov, of blessed memory, has explained that *Your word* which

you uttered, *Let there be a firmament in the midst of the waters...*, these very words and letters [i.e., the Divine creating forces which bring everything into existence *ex nihilo*] stand firmly forever within the firmament of heaven and are forever clothed within all the heavens to give them life, as it is written (Isaiah 40:8), *The word of our L-rd shall stand firm forever....* For if the [creative] letters were to depart [even] for an instant, G-d forbid, and return to their source, all the heavens would become naught and absolute nothingness, and it would be as though they had never existed at all, exactly as before the utterance, *Let there be a firmament.* And so it is with all created things.... If the letters of the 'ten utterances' by which the earth was created during the Six Days of Creation were to depart from it [but] for an instant, G-d forbid, it would revert to naught and absolute nothingness, exactly as before the Six Days of Creation." See also ibid., ch. 11.

sented through substitutions, exchanges, exchanges of exchanges and substitutions of substitutions, as our teacher [Rabbi Schneur Zalman of Liadi[42]], his soul is in Eden, wrote in the second part of *Tanya*.[43]

Now, from the letters that form the word *shemen*, oil, a creation that G-d endowed with the nature of fuel came into being. And from the letters that form the word *chometz*, vinegar, a creation that G-d endowed with the nature not to act as fuel came into being.

Regarding this it says, "He who tells oil to burn will tell vinegar to burn." The change is [not only in the physical substance but also] in the Divine energy that creates the being.[44]

The same is true of the change from something-to-something that took place during the miracles of the Exodus: the change occurred in the Divine energy that creates the being.

CAUSE AND EFFECT

This something-from-something is different than the something-from-something of cause and effect.[45] In the latter case, the cause does not *turn into* the effect. The cause merely generates the revelation of the effect. In the case of intellect and emotions, for example, intellect is the cause and emotions the effect. The intellect does not *become* emotions. The intellect

---

42. Founder of Chabad-Chasidism; author of *Tanya* and *Shulchan Aruch Harav* (1745-1812). Known colloquially as the Alter Rebbe.

43. **Chapters 1 and 12.**
In the first chapter of *Shaar Hayichud Veha'emunah* (the second part of *Tanya*), Rabbi Schneur Zalman of Liadi writes the following: "Although the name אבן (stone) is not mentioned in the 'ten utterances' recorded in the Torah [—how, then, can we say that letters of the 'ten utterances' are vested within a stone?], nevertheless, life-

force flows to the stone from the 'ten utterances' by means of combinations and substitutions of [their] letters, which are transposed in the 'two hundred and thirty-one gates,' either in direct or reverse order,* as is explained in *Sefer Yetzirah* (ch. 2:4-5), so that ultimately the combination of [letters that forms] the name אבן descends from the 'ten utterances,' and is derived from them—and this [combination of letters] is the life-force of the stone." See Appendix I.

---

* The twenty-two letters of the

נִבְרָאִים, וְיֵשׁ שֶׁנִּזְכְּרוּ בְּצֵירוּפִים חֲלוּפִים וּתְמוּרוֹת וְחִלּוּפִים
דְּחִלּוּפִים וּתְמוּרוֹת דִּתְמוּרוֹת, כְּמוֹ שֶׁכָּתַב רַבֵּינוּ נִשְׁמָתוֹ עֵדֶן
בְּחֵלֶק ב׳ בְּתַנְיָא[מו].

וְהִנֵּה מִצֵּירוּפֵי אוֹתִיּוֹת שֶׁמֶן נִבְרָא בְּרִיאָה אֲשֶׁר הַקָּדוֹשׁ
בָּרוּךְ הוּא הִטְבִּיעַ בּוֹ טֶבַע הַהַדְלָקָה, וּמִצֵּירוּפֵי אוֹתִיּוֹת חוֹמֶץ
נִבְרָא בְּרִיאָה אֲשֶׁר הַקָּדוֹשׁ בָּרוּךְ הוּא הִטְבִּיעַ בּוֹ טֶבַע שֶׁאֵינוֹ
דוֹלֵק.

וְעַל זֶה אוֹמֵר מִי שֶׁאָמַר לְשֶׁמֶן וְיַדְלִיק יֹאמַר לְחוֹמֶץ
וְיַדְלִיק, הֲרֵי שֶׁהַשִּׁינוּי הוּא בְּהַכֹּחַ הָאֱלֹקִי הַמְהַוֶּוה אֶת
הַיֵּשׁ.

אֲשֶׁר כֵּן הוּא גַּם בְּהַיֵּשׁ דְּאוֹתוֹת וּמוֹפְתִים דִּיצִיאַת
מִצְרַיִם, שֶׁהַשִּׁינוּי הוּא בְּהַכֹּחַ הָאֱלֹקִי הַמְהַוֶּוה אֶת הַיֵּשׁ.

וְהַיְינוּ שֶׁאֵינוֹ דּוֹמֶה לְיֵשׁ מִיֵּשׁ שֶׁבְּעָלָה וְעָלוּל, דְּהַיֵּשׁ מִיֵּשׁ
שֶׁבְּעָלָה וְעָלוּל הֲרֵי אֵין זֶה שֶׁהָעִילָה נַעֲשָׂה מְצִיאוּת הֶעָלוּל,
כִּי אִם שֶׁהָעִילָה גּוֹרֵם הִתְגַּלּוּת הֶעָלוּל בִּלְבָד. וּכְמוֹ בְּשֵׂכֶל
וּמִדּוֹת, דְּשֵׂכֶל הוּא עִילָה וְהַמִּדּוֹת הֵם עָלוּלִים, הֲרֵי אֵין זֶה

---

44. G-d changes the "letters," i.e., the specific type of Divine energy that is vested within the vinegar, and replaces it with a different Divine energy, that of oil. Hence, "He who *tells*

oil to burn"—i.e., the Divine letters of speech that enliven oil—"will *tell* vinegar to burn."

45. *Ilah v'alul*, in the Hebrew. The relationship between *ilah* and *alul* is such that the *alul* is *contained within* the *ilah*—albeit in an undefined state—even before the *alul* emerges into being. The *ilah produces* the *alul*; it does not *create* it. Thus, the *alul's* emergence is not a creation of a new being, since it is merely a *revelation* from within the *ilah* where it was "hidden," i.e., undefined.

Hebrew alphabet in two-lettered combinations yield a total of 462 combinations. Of these, half are the exact reverse of the other half, e.g., *alef-bet, bet-alef.* Hence, there are 231 two-lettered combinations in direct order and the same number in reverse order.

causes the revelation of an emotion, which is a separate entity.[46]

The same is true of the something-from-something within intellect, i.e., when from one concept another is derived. The first concept does not *become* the second concept. The second concept, which is generated from the first, is a separate entity. It is just that its *emergence* occurs through the first concept.

Not so in the case of the something-from-something of the miracles of the Exodus. Here, the substance of the staff *became* the substance of a snake and the substance of the water *became* the substance of blood. Likewise, in the case of the water that turned into a wall during the splitting of the sea, the change occurred in the Divine energy that creates the being. If so, these miracles are similar to the creation of something-from-nothing.[47]

The truth is, however, that our master [Rabbi Schneur Zalman of Liadi], his soul is in Eden, comes to the conclusion in the second chapter of the second part of *Tanya* that the creation of heaven and earth is a greater miracle [than the splitting of the sea].[48]

---

46. When one contemplates the virtues of something, he will typically begin to feel an emotion toward that thing. The contemplation can thus be termed the "cause," and the ensuing emotion the "effect." Now in this scenario, the intellectual contemplation has not been *transformed into* an emotional feeling. It is not as if his mind has somehow *become* his heart. Rather, his contemplation merely *awakened* these feelings. This is an example of a generation of something-from-something that is clearly different than the creation of something-from-nothing.

47. The discourse has established two points regarding the miracles surrounding the Exodus: 1) The miracles

effected a change in the substance, nature, and ultimately, the very lifeforce, of the respective entities; 2) the miracles actually *transformed* the original entity into the "new" entity (not that the first entity revealed a previously existent second entity). Based on these two points, it would seem that these miracles are of the same sort as the miracle of Creation (something-from-nothing). For since the new entity is of an altogether different substance, nature and life-force than its predecessor, its existence is just as miraculous as that of an entirely new being.

There are two kinds of something-from-something that *do* differ from something-from-nothing: 1) When the second entity is of the same sub-

שֶׁהַשֵּׂכֶל נַעֲשֶׂה מִדּוֹת כִּי אִם אֲשֶׁר הַשֵּׂכֶל גּוֹרֵם הִתְגַּלּוּת הַמִּדָּה שֶׁהִיא מַהוּת בִּפְנֵי עַצְמָהּ.

וְכֵן הוּא בְּיֵשׁ מִיֵּשׁ שֶׁבַּשֵּׂכֶל גּוּפָא, וְהוּא מַה שֶׁמַּשְׂכֵּל אֶחָד יוֹדְעִים עוֹד שֵׂכֶל, הֲרֵי אֵין זֶה שֶׁהַשֵּׂכֶל הָרִאשׁוֹן נַעֲשֶׂה שֵׂכֶל הַשֵּׁנִי כִּי אִם שֶׁהַשֵּׂכֶל הַשֵּׁנִי הַמִּתְהַוֶּוה מִן שֵׂכֶל הָרִאשׁוֹן הוּא מְצִיאוּת בִּפְנֵי עַצְמָהּ, וְרַק דְּהִתְגַּלּוּתוֹ הוּא עַל יְדֵי שֵׂכֶל הָרִאשׁוֹן.

מַה שֶׁאֵין כֵּן בְּיֵשׁ מִיֵּשׁ שֶׁבָּאוֹתוֹת וּמוֹפְתִים דִּיצִיאַת מִצְרַיִם, הוּא שֶׁמִּיֵּשׁ הַמַּטֶּה נֶהְפַּךְ לְיֵשׁ דְּנָחָשׁ וּמֵהַיֵּשׁ דְּמַיִם נֶהְפַּךְ לְיֵשׁ דְּדָם, וְכֵן הוּא גַּם בְּזֶה שֶׁהַמַּיִם נִצְּבוּ כְּמוֹ נֵד בִּקְרִיעַת יַם סוּף, הֲרֵי שֶׁהַשִּׁנּוּי הוּא בְּהַכֹּחַ אֱלֹקִי הַמְהַוֶּוה אֶת הַיֵּשׁ, אִם כֵּן הָוֵי זֶה כְּמוֹ בְּרִיאָה יֵשׁ מֵאַיִן.

אֲבָל בֶּאֱמֶת הִנֵּה רַבֵּינוּ נִשְׁמָתוֹ עֵדֶן, בְּפֶרֶק ב' דְּחֵלֶק ב' בְּתַנְיָא, בָּא לִידֵי מַסְקָנָא דִּבְרִיאַת שָׁמַיִם וָאָרֶץ הוּא פֶּלֶא יוֹתֵר גָּדוֹל.

---

stance as the original entity (albeit in a different form)—such as when a table is crafted from a piece of wood; 2) when the second entity is of a different substance than the original, but does not directly evolve from the original entity—such as in the example of the emotions that emerge from intellectual comprehension (where the emotions have a source independent from the intellect, and are just *revealed* by the intellect).

But, as our discourse explains, the miracles of the Exodus do not fall into either of these two categories. Thus, they are akin to the miracle of Creation—something-from-nothing.

Nevertheless, Rabbi Yosef Yitzchak defers unquestioningly to the opinion of his predecessor, Rabbi Schneur Zalman of Liadi, who considered the creation of heaven and earth to be a greater miracle than the splitting of the sea.

48. See *Shaar Hayichud Veha'emunah*, ch. 2 (cited below, Appendix II).
The reason for this, as explained in the discourse entitled *Hachodesh* in *Sefer Hamaamarim 5679* (p. 324), is because with regards to the miracles of Egypt, both entities—the original, and the newly transformed—were in existence prior to the miracle. Sticks and snakes, water and blood—all of these elements existed previously in the world. Likewise, the second element's "new" nature also existed previously. When the sea split and stood like a wall, the water acquired the *pre-*

If so, why does it say *[I am the L-rd your G-d] who brought you out of the land of Egypt* and not *who created heaven and earth*, which is a greater miracle?[49]

---

viously existent nature of a rigid wall. As Rabbi Schneur Zalman writes there in Tanya: "*For a stone wall stands erect...*"—i.e., such is its created, existent nature. The miracle lies in the fact that water, naturally free-flowing, acquired an entirely different nature, that of a wall—but the water did not acquire a nature that never existed. The miracle of Creation, however, is that from *nothing* there should emerge *something*—for the

אִם כֵּן, לָמָּה נֶאֱמַר אֲשֶׁר הוֹצֵאתִיךָ מֵאֶרֶץ מִצְרַיִם וְלֹא
נֶאֱמַר אֲשֶׁר בָּרָאתִי שָׁמַיִם וָאָרֶץ, שֶׁהוּא פֶּלֶא יוֹתֵר.

---

first time. This, then, is a greater miracle.

49. At the conclusion of chapter 2, we remain with the same issue raised at the conclusion of chapter 1: Which is greater, Nissan or Tishrei; namely, the Exodus or Creation?

On this note, the discourse proceeds to expound the magnitude of Creation.

3.

It is written, *In the beginning G-d (*Elokim*) created....*[50]
The creation of the worlds[51] occurred through the Divine
name *Elokim*, which is the attribute of judgment and *tzimtzum*.[52] For creation of worlds means that they should be independent and limited beings.[53]

Before the creation of the worlds, everything was nullified
to and unified—in the ultimate sense—with the Infinite
Light.[54] They were not independent beings, and not even limited beings. But when the idea arose in His will to create
worlds, they became independent beings.

The truth is that even after the creation of worlds, there is
nothing outside of His Essence.[55] Nevertheless, so it arose in
His will that the world should be an entity that appears independent from Him, and that it should be limited.

As the Talmud says: "From the earth to the [first of the
seven] heavens is a 500-year journey. And the thickness of

---

50. **Genesis 1:1.**

51. I.e., the four worlds of *Atzilut, Beriah, Yetzirah* and *Asiyah* that generally comprise all of created existence.
See Schochet, *Mystical Concepts in
Chassidism*, chapter 4 (*Worlds*) (Kehot, 1988).

52. ELOKIM. One of the seven in-
effable Divine names, *Elokim* is the
primary Divine name used in the Torah's narrative of Creation.
 There are many Hebrew names for
G-d in Scripture, each of which ex-
presses a different aspect or attribute
of the Divinity. *Elokim* denotes G-d
in His attribute of justice (*middat ha-
din*). The fact that the Torah uses
Elokim throughout the narrative of
Creation teaches us that "justice" is
the original state of the world—i.e.,
that man be treated exactly according
to his deeds. G-d, however, saw that

the world could not survive such scru-
tiny, so He tempered His justice with
His attribute of mercy (*middat ha-
rachamim*), the Divine name *Havaya*
(*Rashi*, Genesis 1:1; *Bereishit Rabbah*
12:15; et al.).
 In a deeper sense, Kabbalah and
Chasidus explain that the name
Elokim is vital to Creation itself; in order for there to be Creation, there had
to be *Elokim*, the attribute of justice
and severity. To explain: Prior to
Creation, there was only the infinite
revelation of G-d—the *Or Ein Sof*—
filling all existence. Within this infinite revelation, finite worlds and beings could not possibly exist. When it
arose in G-d's will to create the worlds
and all their inhabitants, He contracted and concealed the *Or Ein Sof*,
creating a "void" within which finite
existence can endure (*Eitz Chaim,
Shaar* 1, a*naf* 3; *Otzrot Chaim*, beg.).
This process is known as *tzimtzum,*

ג.

וְהָעִנְיָן, דְּהִנֵּה כְּתִיב בְּרֵאשִׁית בָּרָא⁵⁴ אֱלֹקִים, דִּבְרִיאַת הָעוֹלָמוֹת הוּא עַל יְדֵי שֵׁם אֱלֹקִים שֶׁהוּא מִדַּת הַדִּין וְהַצִּמְצוּם, דְּהִתְהַוּוּת הָעוֹלָמוֹת הוּא שֶׁיִּהְיוּ מְצִיאוּת דָּבָר נִפְרָד וּבִמְצִיאוּת מוּגְבָּל.

דְּקוֹדֶם שֶׁנִּבְרָא הָעוֹלָם הָיָה הַכֹּל מַדְרֵיגוֹת שֶׁהֵם בְּטֵלִים וּמְיוּחָדִים בְּאוֹר אֵין סוֹף בְּתַכְלִית הַיִּחוּד, וְלֹא הָיוּ בִּבְחִינַת מְצִיאוּת יֵשׁ, וְאַף גַּם לֹא בִּמְצִיאוּת מוּגְבָּל, וּכְשֶׁעָלָה בִּרְצוֹנוֹ יִתְבָּרֵךְ לְהַוּוֹת הָעוֹלָמוֹת נַעֲשׂוּ בִּבְחִינַת מְצִיאוּת יֵשׁ.

וְעִם הֱיוֹת שֶׁגַּם לְאַחַר שֶׁנִּתְהַווּ הָעוֹלָמוֹת הֲרֵי אֵין דָּבָר שֶׁחוּץ לְעַצְמוּתוֹ יִתְבָּרֵךְ, מִכָּל מָקוֹם, הִנֵּה כַּךְ עָלָה בִּרְצוֹנוֹ יִתְבָּרֵךְ, שֶׁיִּהְיֶה הָעוֹלָם בִּבְחִינַת יֵשׁ נִרְאֶה לְנִפְרָד, וּבְהַגְבָּלָה דַּוְקָא.

כְּמַאֲמַר מִן הָאָרֶץ⁵⁵ עַד לָרָקִיעַ מַהֲלַךְ ת"ק שָׁנָה, וְעָבְיוֹ שֶׁל

---

the Self-contraction or Self-limitation of the *Or Ein Sof,* and is an expression of G-d's attribute of justice and severity—embodied in the Divine name *Elokim.*

Thus, *Elokim* represents the aspect of G-d which conceals the Infinite light and life-force, a force that is too intense for finite creatures to endure. *Elokim* is also the power of G-d that makes the world appear as though it exists naturally and independently by itself. *Elokim* therefore has the same numerical value as the Hebrew word for "nature"—*hateva.* See *Shaar Hayichud Veha'emunah,* beg. of ch. 6.

53. And, as explained in the previous footnote, creation of finite beings requires a limiting and contracting—*tzimtzum*—of the *Or Ein Sof,*

G-d's Infinite Light.

54. OR EIN SOF, in the Hebrew.

The Kabbalists use the term *Ein Sof* (lit., "infinite," "endless") to refer to the most absolute Infinite force of G-d, totally beyond description, knowledge, and comprehension, completely beyond any boundaries—the Essence of G-d Himself. G-d's infinite expression and revelation—the *Infinite light*—is termed, in Hebrew, *Or Ein Sof.*

For as to why the mystics chose to refer to the effusion of Divinity as "light," see *Mystical Concepts in Chassidism,* chapter 1 (*Anthropomorphism and Metaphors*), section 3.

55. See *Tanya,* ch. 21; *Shaar Hayichud Veha'emunah,* end of ch. 3.

[each] heaven is a 500-year journey... The feet of the *chayot* [angels] are equal to all of them... The lower parts the legs of the *chayot* [angels] are equal to all of them...."[56]

The Sages also said: "An angel stands in a third of the world."[57]

There are two interpretations of this statement: 1) An angel is the size of a third of the world;[58] and 2) the world is a third of the size of an angel.[59]

[In any event,] although it is an immense measurement, it is also an immense limitation.[60]

SUPERNAL ANGELS

This [limitation] is true of the supernal angels as well, who vary in their Divine perception and their love and awe of the Divine. The *Serafim*[61] say *Kadosh*, Holy, and the *Ofanim* say *Baruch*, Blessed.[62]

---

56. *Chagigah* 13a.

Nebuchadnezzar once said (Isaiah 14:14): *I shall ascend beyond the heights of the clouds; I will be like the Most High.* He wished to reach the highest level, the throne of G-d Himself, and to be a god. A voice from heaven responded to his arrogant ambition, chastising him by pointing out the vastness of creation and the insignificance of mortal man. (Maharal in *Be'er Hagolah, Be'er 6*, understands the Talmud to be referring to the *spiritual* "distance" between one dimension and the next.)

Yet, although the worlds are vast, they are nonetheless defined and limited ("a 500-year journey..."). This demonstrates the finiteness of creation, and thus the necessity for there to be a *tzimtzum* and limiting of the *Or Ein Sof.*

57. *Bereishit Rabbah* 68:12—in different wording. There the expression is: "The angel is a third of the world."

58. *Bereishit Rabbah* ibid.; *Chullin* 91b.

59. **This interpretation is cited also in *Vera'iti Ani 5662* [*Sefer Hamaamarim 5660-62*, p. 350]. For the present, I do not know its source.**

An earlier source has subsequently been published: *Torat Shmuel 5633*, vol. 1, p. 24. In *Sefer Hamaamarim 5708*, p. 280, the Lubavitcher Rebbe, Rabbi Menachem M. Schneerson, notes that in addition to its being cited in the aforementioned discourse of 5662, it is also cited in numerous other places, and "this requires further research."

See also *Sefer Hamaamarim 5699*, p. 211, end: "Both interpretations are true. There are angels as large as a third of the world, and there are angels that are three times the size of the world."

60. In other words, irrespective of how immense the worlds or the angels may be, creation is ultimately finite and limited.

רָקִיעַ מַהֲלַךְ ת"ק שָׁנָה כו׳, רַגְלֵי הַחַיּוֹת כְּנֶגֶד כּוּלָן כו׳, שׁוֹקֵי הַחַיּוֹת כְּנֶגֶד כּוּלָן.

וְאָמְרוּ וּמַלְאָךְ בִּשְׁלִישׁ⁴⁸ עוֹלָם הוּא עוֹמֵד.

וְיֵשׁ בָּזֶה ב׳ פֵּירוּשִׁים, אִם הַמַּלְאָךְ הוּא שְׁלִישׁ הָעוֹלָם⁴⁹ אוֹ שֶׁהָעוֹלָם⁵⁰ הוּא שְׁלִישׁ הַמַּלְאָךְ.

דְּעַם הֱיוֹתוֹ מִדָּה גְדוֹלָה בְּיוֹתֵר, בְּכָל זֶה הוּא הַגְבָלָה בְּיוֹתֵר.

וְכֵן הוּא בְּמַלְאָכִים הָעֶלְיוֹנִים שֶׁהֵם מְחוּלָקִים בְּהַשָּׂגָתָם וּבְהָאַהֲבָה וְיִרְאָה שֶׁלָּהֶם, דִּשְׂרָפִים אוֹמְרִים קָדוֹשׁ וְאוֹפַנִּים⁵¹ אוֹמְרִים בָּרוּךְ.

---

61. SERAFIM and OFANIM. *Serafim* and *Ofanim* are two types of angels mentioned in Scripture (see Isaiah 6:2; Ezekiel 1:15). The *Serafim* reside in the world of *Beriah*, where the Throne of Glory stands... In *Beriah*, *binah* of *Atzilut* (the attribute of Supernal understanding) is manifest; therefore, all the creations of *Beriah* (*Serafim* included) possess great understanding. *Ofanim*, however, reside in the world of *Asiyah*, which is incomparably lower than *Beriah*. The *Serafim* are therefore of a higher stature than *Ofanim*.

[Yet, there is a virtue in the song of the *Ofanim* over that of the *Serafim*, as our Sages said (*Chullin* 91b): "The Children of Israel are more precious than the angels... The Children of Israel mention G-d's name after two words, as in *Shema Yisrael Hashem...*, whereas the angels only mention G-d's name after three words, as in *Kadosh kadosh kadosh Hashem....*" Now, this is true of the *Serafim*; they only mention G-d's name after three words. The *Ofanim*, however do mention G-d's name after two words, when they say *Baruch k'vod Hashem....* This is because the *Ofanim* emanate from a loftier source, the world of *Tohu*, which precedes *Tikkun*. They thus descended to a lower world, in accordance with the rule, "the higher its source, the lower its descent"—similar to a stone that falls off the top row of a wall, which falls further away from the wall than would a stone falling from the bottom row.]

Serafim reside in *Beriah*, for they have been refined and have exited their stance of selfness. But they have not yet been totally subsumed within their Source, the blessed *Ein Sof*, which shines within the world of *Atzilut*. That takes place when they offer their praise to G-d. They are therefore in *Beriah*, a world where goodness dominates.

Ofanim, however, have not yet

It is similarly written, *He acts according to His will with the host of heaven....*[63] The [Divine] worship of [the heavenly angel] Michael is with love, while [the angel] Gabriel's worship is with awe.[64] And although they remain constantly within their mode of worship—this one with love and this one with awe, from which they do not detract and to which they do not add[65]—nevertheless, each one possesses many [spiritual] camps, which differ one from the other.[66]

For the truth is that all of them [the angels] are spiritual entities. It follows, then, that the distinction between them lies [not in anything physical or spatial, but] in their varying modes of worship—Michael with love, Gabriel with awe. This distinction constitutes limitation[67]—each one is limited

---

been refined, and therefore reside in *Asiyah*, a world where evil is the dominating force.

Serafim understand that G-d is "holy" and "separated" from the worlds, because *Beriah* is a world of "understanding," since, as mentioned above, in it is manifest a ray of *binah* of *Atzilut*. Hence they recite "*kadosh*" (holy) three times to signify the three worlds of *Beriah, Yetzirah* and *Asiyah.* (On a more lofty level, this may also refer to the three worlds of *Atzilut, Beriah* and *Yetzirah.*) This comprehension nullifies them to their very essence. Hence their name "*Serafim*"—from the root *saraf,* burn—for their entire being is "burnt" and consumed in this abnegation.

Ofanim hear the *Kadosh* that the *Serafim* say, but they do not comprehend it. Their intellect is too small to contain the comprehension of *Kadosh.* Thus, they "shout with a mighty sound"—similar to man who hears something but does not understand it, and noisily asks, "What is this?!" The *Ofanim* likewise act in this manner when they hear the *Kadosh*

recited by the *Serafim.* Another reason for their "mighty sound" is because, as mentioned above, they originate from *Tohu,* a realm where the spiritual light was too intense to be controlled or contained (*Sefer Hamaamarim 5688,* pp. 97-99).

62. **Chullin 92a.**

KADOSH and BARUCH: *Serafim* recite *Kadosh* for they are in a mode of ascent; by terming something "holy" one refers to something greater, higher, more lofty. Conversely, *Ofanim* recite *Baruch*—which connotes eliciting downward—for their duty is to elicit G-dly revelation below (*Or Hatorah, Massei,* p. 1356).

(*Bracha* has the connotation of *hamshacha* (drawing downward), from the term in *Kilayim* 7:1, "*Hamavrich et hagefen*"—one who grafts a vine, by bending its top downwards back into the ground and bringing the top back out of the ground.)

63. **Daniel 4:32.** This verse further underscores the fact that even the supernal angels are created with lim-

וּכְתִיב וּכְמִצְבְּיֵהּ עָבֵידᵏᵇ בְּחֵיל שְׁמַיָּא, דְּמִיכָאֵל עֲבוֹדָתוֹᵏᵍ
בְּאַהֲבָה וְגַבְרִיאֵל עֲבוֹדָתוֹ בְּיִרְאָה, וַהֲגַם שֶׁהֵם עוֹמְדִים תָּמִיד
כָּל אֶחָד מֵהֶם בַּעֲבוֹדָתוֹ, זֶה בְּאַהֲבָה וְזֶה בְּיִרְאָה, דְּמִמֶּנּוּ לֹא
יִגְרַע וְעָלָיו לֹא יוֹסִיף, מִכָּל מָקוֹם הִנֵּה כָּל אֶחָד מֵהֶם יֵשׁ לוֹ
רִיבּוּי מַחֲנוֹת שֶׁהֵם חֲלוּקִים זֶה מִזֶּה.

דְּבֶאֱמֶת הֲלֹא כּוּלָּם הֵם מְצִיאוּת רוּחָנִי, אִם כֵּן הִתְחַלְּקוּתָם
זֶה מִזֶּה הוּא בְּאוֹפֶן עֲבוֹדָתָם, בְּאַהֲבָה בְּמַחֲנֵה מִיכָאֵל וּבְיִרְאָה
בְּמַחֲנֵה גַבְרִיאֵל, דְּהִתְחַלְּקוּת זֹאת הוּא עִנְיַן הַהַגְבָּלָה, מַה

---

itation and finiteness. For, as the discourse will soon explain, the supernal angels are distinguished from each other by their particular, distinct mode of worshipping G-d. And distinction is synonymous with limitation; they are *distinct* in their mode of worship because they are *limited* to that very mode. Thus, *He acts according to His will with the host of heaven....*: G-d created limited, finite angels, to serve Him each in their own particular way.

64. See *Likkutei Torah, Bamidbar,* s.v. *U'sefartem* and its explanation, et al. [10a].

Likkutei Torah, ibid.: "Each camp of angels ascends differently, according to its level. Each one's level is separate and distinct from its fellow's, as the verse says (Ezekiel 1:10), *The face of the lion to the right,* i.e., with love—this is the camp of Michael. *And the face of the ox*—this is the camp of Gabriel—*to the left,* with awe."

65. See *Likkutei Torah,* ibid., 10b: "The angels are called 'stationary,' since they stay on the same [spiritual]

level throughout their entire existence, without any diminishment, addition or change [to their Divine service]."

66. *Likkutei Torah,* ibid., 11b: "The camp of Michael, for example, which is the camp of *chesed,* kindness, includes within it *chesed* of *chesed* of *chesed,* or *chesed* of *gevurah* of *chesed.* Although they are all from one attribute—*chesed*—there are nonetheless many facets of *chesed,* and these are represented in the myriad of angels in each camp. So although the camp of Michael includes within it elements of all the ten *sefirot,* it is still called *chesed* since the *sefirah* of *chesed* is the main attribute among them."

All of this demonstrates the vast distinction and finiteness of the angels (and all of creation), which stems from the limitation and *tzimtzum* of the Infinite Light—*Elokim.*

67. The fact that such multiplicity exists within creation demonstrates how *limited* creation is; for it is a thing's limitations that ultimately defines what it is and distinguishes it from something else.

to its mode of worship. And limitation is incomparable to the Infinite Light, which is unlimited.

The creation of the worlds, therefore, required at its root the attribute of *malchut*,[68] kingship.[69] This idea is expressed in the verse, *Your kingship (*malchut*) is a kingship (*malchut*) over all worlds*[70]—i.e., the creation of all worlds stems from the attribute of *malchut*.

The same idea is expressed in the phrase, "You are the only One—the life of [all] the worlds, O King"[71]: to proceed from the Infinite Light, which is "One" and Unique, to "life of [all] the worlds," requires the attribute of "King"—*malchut*.

MALCHUT

Malchut is distinct from all of the other supernal *sefirot*.[72]

This can be understood through the metaphor of the attributes of the soul.[73] Take the attribute of *chesed*, kindness, for example; its essence can exist even without a recipient of the kindness. One who is inherently a good person possesses goodness and kindness in his heart; and when someone is in need of his assistance he gives him of his goodness and kindness.

---

68. MALCHUT. Lit., "royalty" or "kingship," *malchut* is the tenth and last of the *sefirot*. *Malchut* is referred to in the *Tikkunei Zohar* (intro. 17a) as the "mouth of G-d," the word or speech of G-d by which the worlds come into actual being (see above, ch. 2 and footnote 41). Indeed, it is the creation of the worlds that makes it possible to speak of a Divine kingdom, since, as the discourse will later say, "There cannot be a King without a nation"—G-d cannot be a "ruler" without there existing something to rule over (see, however, below, ch. 6).

Malchut, being the "lowest" of the ten *sefirot*, is referred to in *Eitz Chaim* (6:5, 8:5, et passim) as being "a dim reflector, because it has no (light) of its own." The *Zohar* (I:249b, 251b) therefore compares *malchut* to "the

moon that has no light of its own save that which is given to it from the sun." Paradoxically, although *malchut* is a passive sphere that only contains that which the other *sefirot* pour into it, it is specifically through *malchut* that the original creative plan is actualized. But *malchut* can only actualize the potential of the earlier *sefirot*.

Malchut's specific role in the creation of the worlds will be discussed at length in this discourse (chapters 3-6).

69. As the discourse just demonstrated, creation is defined by multiplicity and limitation. It follows, then, that the *sefirah* of *malchut* plays a vital role in the creative process, as *malchut* is the lowest of the ten *sefirot*, and allows for and embodies limitation. This point will be explained in great detail

שֵׂכֶל אֶחָד מֵהֶם מוּגְבָּל בְּאוֹתָהּ הָעֲבוֹדָה שֶׁהוּא בָהּ, וּגְבוּל הוּא בְּאֵין עֲרוֹךְ לְגַבֵּי אוֹר אֵין סוֹף הַבְּלִי גְבוּל.

אֲשֶׁר עַל כֵּן, הִנֵּה בִּכְדֵי שֶׁיִּהְיֶה הִתְהַוּוּת הָעוֹלָמוֹת, הִנֵּה הַמָּקוֹר לָזֶה הוּא מִדַּת הַמַּלְכוּת, כְּמוֹ שֶׁכָּתוּב מַלְכוּתְךָ מַלְכוּת[עד] כָּל עוֹלָמִים, דְּכָל עוֹלָמִים הִנֵּה הִתְהַוּוּתָם הוּא מִבְּחִינַת מַלְכוּת.

וּכְמַאֲמַר יָחִיד חֵי[עה] הָעוֹלָמִים מֶלֶךְ, דְּמֵאוֹר אֵין סוֹף שֶׁהוּא בְּחִינַת יָחִיד וּמְיוּחָד, שֶׁיִּהְיֶה חֵי הָעוֹלָמִים שֶׁהוּא חַיּוּת הָעוֹלָמוֹת, הוּא עַל יְדֵי מֶלֶךְ בְּחִינַת מַלְכוּת.

שֶׁבַּסְּפִירוֹת הָעֶלְיוֹנוֹת הִנֵּה סְפִירַת הַמַּלְכוּת חֲלוּקָה מִשְּׁאָרֵי הַסְּפִירוֹת.

וְיוּבַן זֶה מִכֹּחוֹת הַנֶּפֶשׁ, דְּבְמִדַּת הַחֶסֶד הִנֵּה עֶצֶם הַמִּדָּה יְכוֹלָה שֶׁתִּהְיֶה גַּם בְּלִי זוּלַת שֶׁמְּקַבֵּל אֶת הַחֶסֶד, דְּמִי שֶׁהוּא אִישׁ טוֹב בְּעֶצֶם הֲרֵי יֵשׁ בּוֹ הַטּוֹב וְהַחֶסֶד בְּלִבּוֹ, וּכְשֶׁיִּהְיֶה מִי שֶׁנִּצְרָךְ לוֹ הִנֵּה יַשְׁפִּיעַ[עו] לוֹ מֵחַסְדּוֹ וְטוּבוֹ.

---

below, where the discourse highlights the uniqueness of *malchut*, and how it differs from the other *sefirot*.

70. **Psalms 145:13.**

71. Liturgy, *Baruch She'amar*.

72. SEFIROT. There are ten creative Divine attributes and manifestations of G-d, called *sefirot*. These are: *chochmah* (wisdom), *binah* (understanding), *daat* (knowledge), *chesed* (kindness), *gevurah* (severity), *tiferet* (beauty), *netzach* (victory), *hod* (splendor), *yesod* (foundation) and *malchut* (kingship). The *sefirot* are divided into two categories: the first three are *sechel* (intellectual attributes), the latter seven *middot* (emotive attributes). The ten *sefirot* manifest themselves in each

of the four spiritual worlds, and are the source of (and parallel to) the ten powers of the human soul. Just as man reveals himself through his attributes, or their "garments" (thought, speech and deed), similarly G-d reveals Himself through His attributes, the *sefirot*. See *Mystical Concepts in Chassidism*, chapter 3 (*Sefirot*).

73. As mentioned in the previous footnote, the ten supernal *sefirot* are mirrored in the ten attributes or powers of the soul. Examining the soul's attributes can therefore shed light on their cosmic counterparts. In man, the attribute of *malchut* refers to one's feeling of exaltedness (or dominion) over others.

Even the animation of the attribute of kindness can occur without the presence of a beneficiary.[74] For example, Abraham our forefather was constantly animated with kindness, such that when [after his circumcision] G-d brought scorching heat upon the world[75]—so that Abraham would not be burdened with guests—Abraham was distressed[76] [because of the lack of travelers to invite to his tent]. His distress was due to the fact that he was constantly animated with the quality of kindness.[77]

The same is true of all of the soul's attributes. The *implementation* of the attribute cannot take place without another being upon whom the attribute can be implemented and who will receive the [effect of] the feeling. But the essence of the attribute—and even the animation of the attribute—can exist without a recipient of the attribute itself and its animation.

But with *malchut*, which is the power of exaltedness within the soul, although it is only a power like the soul's other powers—i.e., it exists within the soul just as the other powers exist there—nevertheless, the essence of the attribute and power of exaltedness, as well as its animation, cannot exist without the presence of another being. This can be empirically observed: If a person is in a barren desert without any other human present he will not be animated by an element of exaltedness. This distinguishes the quality of exaltedness from the other attributes.[78]

---

74. In other words, not only does the attribute of kindness exist within a good person in a *dormant* manner when there is no recipient, it can even be *animated* within the person, as the discourse now illustrates.

75. *Bava Metzia* 86b: "G-d removed the sun from its sheath." See *Bereishit Rabbah* 48:8: "G-d pierced a hole in Gehinom (Purgatory) and heated the entire world and its inhabitants for a

short while. He said: 'The righteous are in pain and the world is comfortable?' For, indeed, heat is beneficial for [healing] a wound." As *Rashi* explains there, "Better that the world should be discomforted for a short while so that Abraham can benefit from the extreme heat."

76. *Rashi, Vayeira* [Genesis 18:1].

77. Obviously, without wayfarers,

וְגַם הַתְעוֹרְרוּת מִדַּת הַחֶסֶד יְכוֹלָה לִהְיוֹת בְּלִי זוּלַת, וּכְמוֹ אַבְרָהָם אָבִינוּ עָלָיו הַשָּׁלוֹם, הֲרֵי הָיָה תָּמִיד בְּהִתְעוֹרְרוּת בְּחֶסֶד, וּכְשֶׁהִרְתִּיחוֹ הַקָּדוֹשׁ בָּרוּךְ הוּא אֶת הָעוֹלָם שֶׁלֹּא לְהַטְרִיחוֹ בְּאוֹרְחִים, הָיָה בְּצַעֲרוֹ מִזֶּה, לְפִי שֶׁתָּמִיד עָמַד בְּהִתְעוֹרְרוּת דְּמִדַּת הַחֶסֶד.

וְכֵן הוּא בְּכָל מִדָּה וּמִדָּה מִמִּדּוֹת הַנֶּפֶשׁ, שֶׁעִם הֱיוֹת דִּפְעוּלַת הַמִּדָּה הֲרֵי אִי אֶפְשָׁר בְּלֹא זוּלַת עַל מִי שֶׁתִּתְפַּשֵּׁט הַמִּדָּה הַהִיא וּמִי שֶׁיְּקַבֵּל הַמִּדָּה, אֲבָל עֶצֶם הַמִּדָּה וְכֵן אֲפִילוּ הִתְעוֹרְרוּת הַמִּדָּה, הֲרֵי יְכוֹלִים לִהְיוֹת גַּם בְּלֹא זוּלַת עַל מִי שֶׁתִּהְיֶה הָעֶצֶם וְהִתְעוֹרְרוּת שֶׁל הַמִּדָּה.

אֲבָל בְּמִדַּת הַמַּלְכוּת שֶׁהוּא כֹּחַ הַהִתְנַשְּׂאוּת שֶׁבַּנֶּפֶשׁ, עִם הֱיוֹתָהּ גַּם כֵּן רַק כֹּחַ כְּמוֹ שְׁאָרֵי כֹּחוֹת הַנֶּפֶשׁ, הַיְינוּ שֶׁנִּמְצֵאת הַמִּדָּה בְּהַנֶּפֶשׁ כְּמוֹ שֶׁשְּׁאָרֵי הַמִּדּוֹת נִמְצָאִים, וּמִכָּל מָקוֹם הִנֵּה עֶצֶם הַמִּדָּה וְהַכֹּחַ דְּהִתְנַשְּׂאוּת וְכֵן הַהִתְעוֹרְרוּת דְּהִתְנַשְּׂאוּת הֲרֵי אִי אֶפְשָׁר לִהְיוֹת בְּלִי זוּלַת. וּכְמוֹ שֶׁאָנוּ רוֹאִים בְּמוּחָשׁ, דְּמִי שֶׁהוּא נִמְצָא בְּמִדְבָּר שָׁמֵם שֶׁאֵין שָׁם אֲנָשִׁים, לֹא יִתְעוֹרֵר בְּמִדַּת הַהִתְנַשְּׂאוּת, הֲרֵי דִּבְזֶה חֲלוּקָה מִדַּת הַהִתְנַשְּׂאוּת מִשְּׁאָרֵי הַמִּדּוֹת.

Abraham was unable to *implement* his faculty of kindness. Nonetheless, this attribute was fully animated *internally*, to the extent that its lack of implementation pained him greatly.

78. By its very definition, *malchut*, the power of exaltedness, means exalted *over others*; there must be others over which to feel exalted. Without the presence of others one will not feel— even internally—any exaltedness. Not so with the other attributes: they exist internally, and can be animated within a person, even when no one else is present.

This distinction between the other attributes and *malchut*—namely, that the other attributes relate to *oneself* while *malchut* relates to *others*—will be the primary focus of the discourse over the next three chapters, as it is the key to understanding why it is specifically the supernal *sefirah* of *malchut* that is associated with the creation of the worlds ("*others*").

4.

The powers and attributes of the soul exist in latent form as well.[79] That is, even the revealed powers exist in latent form as well. It is not that "here they are found; here they were."[80] Rather, they exist in latent form as well.[81]

By this we are not referring to the hidden powers[82] of the soul. The latter refers to the essence of each power and attribute. The idea that all powers and attributes exist in latent form is a separate concept, aside from the concept of the hidden powers.[83]

And here too,[84] the attribute of *malchut*, which is the power of exaltedness, differs from all of the other attributes and powers. Although it too is only an attribute and power—and not the essence of the soul[85]—nevertheless, it differs from the other powers and attributes.

All of the attributes exist [in their latent state] in "a latency that is disposed to revelation"; however, the power of

---

79. In the previous chapter, the Rebbe pointed out one difference between *malchut* and the soul's other attributes; namely, that *malchut* can only exist and be animated within the person after other people awaken within him this feeling of exaltedness, whereas the other attributes exist and can even be animated without the presence of others. In this chapter, the Rebbe traces the origin of this distinction, demonstrating how in its latency *malchut* differs from the other attributes.

80. See *Ketubot* 75b. This expression refers to something that exists constantly in the same state of being; the way it is now is the way it always was. Here, the discourse is saying that this is not true of the soul's attributes. The attributes that are now revealed and manifest within the person existed previously in a *latent* state. It is this latent state of the attributes that

the discourse now examines.

81. This latency refers to the state of the soul-powers prior to their animation. To better understand this, let us examine the faculty of sight. Though it is not one of the ten soul-powers, it may help illustrate what is meant by "latency." When a person's eyes are closed, he still possesses the faculty of sight; he is just not actively using this faculty. So when a person does open his eyes, it is not that he is suddenly acquiring the ability to see; that ability existed—in a state of latency—all along. The same is true of the ten soul-powers. They each exist in latent form prior to their actualization within the person. A person possesses the attribute of kindness, for example, even when it is not actively animated within him.

82. KOCHOT HANE'ELAMIM, in the He-

ו.

וְהִנֵּה כֹּחוֹת וּמִדּוֹת שֶׁבַּנֶּפֶשׁ, הֲרֵי יֵשׁ כְּמוֹ שֶׁהֵם בְּהֶעְלֵם,
שֶׁגַּם כֹּחוֹת הַגְּלוּיִים יֶשְׁנָם כְּמוֹ שֶׁהֵם בְּהֶעְלֵם, וְהַיְינוּ שֶׁאֵין זֶה
שֶׁכַּאן נִמְצְאוּ כַּאן הָיוּ, אֶלָּא שֶׁיֶּשְׁנָם כְּמוֹ שֶׁהֵם בְּהֶעְלֵם.

וְאֵין זֶה שֶׁהֵם כֹּחוֹת הַנֶּעְלָמִים שֶׁבַּנֶּפֶשׁ, שֶׁהַכֹּחוֹת הַנֶּעְלָמִים
הוּא הָעַצְמוּת שֶׁל כָּל כֹּחַ וּמִדָּה, וְעִנְיָן מַה שֶּׁכָּל הַכֹּחוֹת וְהַמִּדּוֹת
יֶשְׁנָם כְּמוֹ שֶׁהֵם בְּהֶעְלֵם הוּא לְבַד עִנְיָנָם שֶׁל כֹּחוֹת הַנֶּעְלָמִים.

הִנֵּה גַם בְּעִנְיָן זֶה הִנֵּה מִדַּת הַמַּלְכוּת שֶׁהוּא כֹּחַ
הַהִתְנַשְּׂאוּת חָלוּק מִכָּל הַמִּדּוֹת וְהַכֹּחוֹת, וְהַיְינוּ, דְּעִם הֱיוֹת
גַּם הִיא אֵינָהּ אֶלָּא מִדָּה וְכֹחַ בִּלְבָד וְאֵינָהּ עֶצֶם הַנֶּפֶשׁ, וּמִכָּל
מָקוֹם הִיא חֲלוּקָה מִשְּׁאָרֵי הַכֹּחוֹת וְהַמִּדּוֹת.

שֶׁכָּל הַמִּדּוֹת הֵם בְּהֶעְלֵם הַשַּׁיָּיךְ אֶל הַגִּילוּי, וְכֹחַ

---

brew. Generally speaking, there are two kinds of *kochot*, soul-powers: there are revealed soul-powers (*kochot hageluyim*) and hidden soul-powers (*kochot hane'elamim*). Revealed soul-powers refers to the dimension of the soul-powers that is perceptible to us and that we experience, whereas hidden soul-powers refers to the essence of the soul-powers that lies deep within the soul, which is not ordinarily manifest or even experienced. Here, the Rebbe specifies that the current discussion will be limited to the revealed soul-powers and their latent and manifest states; he will not be referring to the hidden soul-powers, which are of a different sort altogether. (For more on the hidden soul-powers, see *Sefer Hamaamarim 5703*, p. 157.)

83. As explained in the previous foot-note, hidden soul-powers refers to the soul-powers as they exist within their essence-state—a state that under normal circumstances cannot be revealed. They are thus referred to as *hidden* soul-powers. *Latent* soul-powers, on the other hand, refer to the soul-powers that *can* become manifest, but as they are in a state of latency that precedes revelation and animation.

84. I.e., in the latent state of the powers and attributes of the soul.

85. *Malchut's* latency, as the discourse will soon explain, is deeper and more severe than the other soul-powers. The Rebbe therefore stresses that this being said, *malchut* is still not the *essence* of the soul, but just a soul-power (albeit a unique kind of soul-power).

malchut, which is the power of exaltedness, exists within an even deeper latency [as shall soon be explained].

So the power of exaltedness is equal to the other powers and attributes in the fact that it also exists among the hidden powers.[86] When we say that it differs from the other powers—in that its latency is a deeper one—we are not referring to its hidden power. We are referring to it as it exists in latent form [prior to its revelation].

There is a difference between a hidden power and the latent form of a power. The latter refers to a latency that precedes revelation. For every revelation is preceded by a state of latency; and it is to this latency that we refer when we talk about the latent form of a power.

The hidden power, by contrast, refers to the essence of the power. This hidden power is not disposed to revelation through straightforward means.

So when we say that the attribute of exaltedness differs from the other attributes we are referring to its state of latency that precedes revelation. For all attributes exist in a latent form that is disposed to revelation. And the same is true of the attribute of *malchut*, which is the power of exaltedness. It too exists in a latent form that precedes and is disposed to revelation. But its latency is of another sort.

COAL AND FLINT

It is known[87] that there are two kinds of latency: 1) Where the latent element is in existence; 2) where the latent element is *not* in existence.

Although both are forms of latency, they nonetheless differ in their very essence, and therefore differ in their character and properties.

[To explain:] An "apparent entity" and a "hidden entity" are distinct realities, each one possessing its own character and properties.

---

86. I.e., as the soul-powers exist in their essence-state, as explained above (footnote 82).

87. See *Ve'avraham Zaken 5666* [*Yom Tov Shel Rosh Hashanah 5666*, p. 78]; **Bayom Hashemini Atzeret**

הַמְּלוּכָה, שֶׁהוּא כֹּחַ הַהִתְנַשְּׂאוּת, הוּא בְּהֶעְלֵם פְּנִימִי יוֹתֵר.

וְהַיְינוּ, דְּכֹחַ הַהִתְנַשְּׂאוּת הוּא מִשְׁתַּוֶּוה לִשְׁאָרֵי הַכֹּחוֹת וְהַמִּדּוֹת שֶׁגַּם הוּא נִמְצָא בֵּין כֹּחוֹת הַנֶּעֱלָמִים, וְזֶה מַה שֶׁאוֹמְרִים דְּכֹחַ הַהִתְנַשְּׂאוּת חָלוּק מִשְׁאָרֵי הַכֹּחוֹת, שֶׁהוּא בְּהֶעְלֵם פְּנִימִי יוֹתֵר, אֵין הַכַּוָּונָה עַל הַכֹּחַ נֶעְלָם דְּכֹחַ הַהִתְנַשְּׂאוּת, כִּי אִם הַכַּוָּונָה עַל הַכֹּחַ כְּמוֹ שֶׁהוּא בְּהֶעְלֵם.

דְּיֵשׁ הֶפְרֵשׁ בֵּין כֹּחַ נֶעְלָם לְהַכֹּחַ כְּמוֹ שֶׁהוּא בְּהֶעְלֵם, דְּהַכֹּחַ כְּמוֹ שֶׁהוּא בְּהֶעְלֵם הַכַּוָּונָה עַל הָעְלֵם שֶׁקּוֹדֶם הַגִּילּוּי, דְּכָל גִּילּוּי הֲרֵי קְדָמוֹ הַהֶעְלֵם, הִנֵּה דַרְגָּא זוֹ הוּא מַה שֶׁהַכֹּחַ הוּא בְּהֶעְלֵם.

וְעִנְיַן כֹּחַ נֶעְלָם הוּא הָעַצְמוּת שֶׁל הַכֹּחַ, דְּבְאוֹפֶן יָשָׁר אֵינוֹ שַׁיָּיךְ אֶל הַגִּילּוּי.

וּמַה שֶׁכֹּחַ הַהִתְנַשְּׂאוּת חָלוּק מִשְׁאָרֵי הַמִּדּוֹת הוּא בְּהַהֶעְלֵם שֶׁקּוֹדֶם אֶל הַגִּילּוּי, דְּכָל הַמִּדּוֹת יֶשְׁנָם בְּהָעְלֵם הַשַּׁיָּיךְ אֶל הַגִּילּוּי, אֲשֶׁר כֵּן הוּא גַם בְּמִדַּת הַמַּלְכוּת שֶׁהוּא כֹּחַ הַהִתְנַשְּׂאוּת דְּיֶשְׁנוֹ בְּהֶעְלֵם שֶׁקְּדָם וְשַׁיָּיךְ אֶל הַגִּילּוּי, אֲבָל הַהֶעְלֵם בְּעַצְמוֹ הוּא בְּאוֹפֶן אַחֵר.

דְּיָדוּעַ שֶׁיֵּשׁ[כח] ב׳ בְּחִינוֹת וּמַדְרֵיגוֹת בְּהֶעְלֵם, הָא׳ הָעְלֵם שֶׁיֶּשְׁנוֹ בִּמְצִיאוּת, וְהַב׳ הֶעְלֵם שֶׁאֵינוֹ בִּמְצִיאוּת.

דְּעִם הֱיוֹת שֶׁשְּׁנֵיהֶם הֵם הֶעְלֵם, אֲבָל עִם זֶה הֲרֵי הֵם חֲלוּקִים בְּעֶצֶם מַהוּתָם, וּבְמֵילָא הֲרֵי הֵם חֲלוּקִים בְּהַגְדָּרִים וְהָעִנְיָנִים שֶׁלָּהֶם.

דִּמְצִיאוּת גָּלוּי וּמְצִיאוּת נֶעְלָם הֵם שְׁנֵי מַהוּתִים נִבְדָּלִים, אֲשֶׁר כָּל אֶחָד מֵהֶם יֵשׁ לוֹ גִּדְרוֹ וְעִנְיָנוֹ.

5689 [*Sefer Hamaamarim 5689*, p. 56].

Take fire, for example. There are two types of fire. And while both types are equally fire, they differ in their latency that precedes revelation.

Let us use the example of the fire of coal and the fire of flint.[88] Both fires are of the same sort; there is no difference between fire that emerges from coal and fire that emerges from flint. But this sameness exists only once the fire becomes manifest. At that point, there is no difference between the fire of coal and that of flint.

But they differ dramatically in their latent state. The fire of coal, even in its latent state, is an "*apparent* entity." It is concealed only on the surface of the coal. But within the coal, it exists, and is an "apparent entity."[89]

But the fire of flint—even as it exists within the flint—[is a "hidden entity"].[90] The fire does in fact exist, for it has already been created. It is not as if it only comes into existence when the fire is derived from the flint. If that were the case, it would be called a *creation* [of fire], not a *revelation* [of fire]. The extraction of fire from the flint is the revelation of the concealed, not a creation, since the fire has already been created and is already in existence.[91] Nevertheless, the fire of flint, even in its latent state, is a "hidden entity."[92]

---

88. Fire can be extracted from both a hot coal and a piece of flint. The discourse now examines the difference between how the fire exists in a latent manner within coal and how it exists in a latent manner within flint.

89. The fire actually burns within the coal, where it exists and is "apparent." It is just on the surface of the coal that this fire is not visible.

90. Unlike hot coal, cold, hard flint does not contain within itself a burning fire.

91. This refers to the (spiritual) Ele-

ment of Fire that exists within flint (see following footnote). There is, however, no actual fire within flint.

92. In the case of the coal, the fire is hidden only as far as *we* are concerned; *we* cannot see it. But as far as the fire itself, it is not hidden; it is an "apparent entity" within the coal. The fire in the coal is fully present within the coal—just not on the surface. In the case of the flint, however, it is not just that *we* cannot see the fire; *there is no revealed fire to see*. Even in its latency it is a "hidden entity." Its concealment is therefore real, and not just the result of our perception.

וְעַל דֶּרֶךְ מָשָׁל אֵשׁ, הֲרֵי יֵשׁ ב' סוּגֵי אֵשׁ, דִּשְׁנֵיהֶם הֵם אֵשׁ, אֲבָל עִם זֶה הֲרֵי הֵם חֲלוּקִים בְּעִנְיַן הֶעְלֵמָם שֶׁקּוֹדֵם אֶל הַגִּילּוּי.

וּכְמוֹ אֵשׁ שֶׁבַּגַּחֶלֶת וְאֵשׁ דְּצוּר הַחַלָּמִישׁ, דִּשְׁנֵיהֶם הֵם סוּג אֶחָד דְּאֵשׁ, שֶׁאֵין הֶפְרֵשׁ כְּלָל בֵּין אִם הוּא אֵשׁ הַגַּחֶלֶת לְאֵשׁ דְּצוּר הַחַלָּמִישׁ, אָמְנָם הַשְׁתַּוּוּת זוֹ הִיא רַק כַּאֲשֶׁר בָּאִים בְּהִתְגַּלּוּת, דְּכַאֲשֶׁר הֵם בָּאִים בְּגִילּוּי אָז אֵין הֶפְרֵשׁ בֵּין אֵשׁ הַגַּחֶלֶת לְאֵשׁ הַצּוּר.

אֲבָל בְּאוֹפֶן מְצִיאוּתָם כְּמוֹ שֶׁהֵם בְּהֶעְלֵמָם, הֲרֵי יֵשׁ הֶפְרֵשׁ גָּדוֹל בֵּינֵיהֶם. דְּאֵשׁ הַגַּחֶלֶת הוּא מְצִיאוּת גָּלוּי בְּהֶעְלֵמוֹ, דְּזֶה מַה שֶׁהָאֵשׁ הוּא בְּהֶעְלֵם הוּא כְּלַפֵּי חוּץ מֵהַגַּחֶלֶת, אֲבָל בְּתוֹךְ הַגַּחֶלֶת הוּא בִּמְצִיאוּת וּבְמְצִיאוּת גְּלוּיָה.

וְהָאֵשׁ שֶׁבַּצּוּר, הִנֵּה גַּם כְּמוֹ שֶׁהוּא נִמְצָא בַּצּוּר, הֲגַם שֶׁבֶּאֱמֶת יֶשְׁנוֹ בִּמְצִיאוּת, שֶׁהֲרֵי כְּבָר נִבְרָא, דְּאֵין זֶה דְּבִשְׁעָה שֶׁמּוֹצִיאִין אֶת הָאֵשׁ מִצּוּר הַחַלָּמִישׁ אֲזַי הוּא נִבְרָא, דְּאִם כֵּן הָיָה נוֹפֵל עָלָיו הַלָּשׁוֹן בְּרִיאָה וְלֹא גִילּוּי, וְהוֹצָאַת הָאֵשׁ מֵהַצּוּר הוּא גִילּוּי הַהֶעְלֵם וְלֹא בְּרִיאָה, לְפִי שֶׁהָאֵשׁ כְּבָר נִבְרָא וְיֶשְׁנוֹ בִּמְצִיאוּת, אֶלָּא שֶׁהוּא מְצִיאוּת נֶעֱלָמִי גַּם כְּמוֹ שֶׁהוּא בְּהֶעְלֵמוֹ.

In *Ve'avraham Zaken* cited above, Rabbi Shalom DovBer of Lubavitch writes (pp. 80-81): "Although flint possesses the power of heat from the [spiritual] Element of Fire, which is why it has the capacity to produce fire, nevertheless, it does not contain actual fire at all. The heat that it possesses exists in a very concealed and ethereal form to the extent that there is no perceptible heat at all. In other words, it does not possess actual heat. It is only through striking the flint with iron that the 'spiritual' power of fire that it contains in concealed form emerges. But the fire of coal, even as it exists within the coal, invisible to the outside, contains actual fire, which is invisible and later becomes revealed.

"There are two distinctions between the two fires. Firstly, they differ in the manner in which the fire is extracted. The fire of coal is extracted quite easily while the fire of flint requires much effort. However, the fire of coal is limited and will eventually die out. The fire of flint, by contrast, never dies out, and one can forever continue to extract new fire from it. This, then, is the second difference between them: the fire of coal is limited, whereas the fire of flint is unlimited.

"These distinctions are based on the specific manner in which the fire

The fire of coal therefore emerges on its own and with ease. The fire of flint, by contrast, not only does not become revealed on its own and must be extracted, but moreover this extraction requires forceful effort.[93]

A similar difference lies between the other attributes and the attribute of exaltedness.[94] All the other attributes can be animated even by something that is not in their class. For example, the many animals of Nineveh constituted a cause for mercy.[95]

The attribute of exaltedness, however, can be animated only by another being and one that is in the same class. If a person were to have millions of animals and birds he would not become animated with the attribute of exaltedness. Only a fellow human can awaken this attribute.[96]

---

exists in its respective source. The coal contains actual fire. The extraction of the coal's fire from a hidden state to a revealed state is therefore similar to the emergence of something-from-something, and is therefore done with ease. The flint, however, does not contain actual fire at all. The fire of flint is like a potential power—much like the [spiritual] Element of Fire, which, while itself is not fire, is the potential power for all fire. The extraction of fire from flint is therefore like the emergence of something-from-nothing, and therefore requires much effort....

"This is the difference between an object that exists in concealment and existential concealment. There is a limit to the revelation of the former.

Because it exists in actuality, it is limited. When its power is spent, its revelations automatically cease. But existential concealment, which possesses no actuality at all, and is concealed even from itself, is limitless."

93. The specific manner in which the fire lies latent determines just how easily it will ultimately emerge. The fire of coal emerges with ease, since even in its latency within the coal the fire is an "apparent entity." The fire of flint, conversely, which in its latency is a "hidden entity," emerges only with force.

94. The discourse now applies the aforementioned concept to man's attributes.

וְלָכֵן אֵשׁ הַגַּחֶלֶת יוֹצֵא בְּעַצְמוֹ מֵהֶעְלֵם אֶל הַגִּילוּי
וּבְנָקֵל, וְהָאֵשׁ שֶׁבַּצוּר הִנֵּה לֹא זוֹ בִּלְבָד שֶׁמֵּעַצְמוֹ לֹא
יִתְגַּלֶּה וּצְרִיכִים לְהוֹצִיאוֹ, הִנֵּה גַּם זֶה הוּא עַל יְדֵי יְגִיעָה
בְּכֹחַ דַּוְקָא.

דְּכֵן הוּא הַהֶפְרֵשׁ בֵּין שְׁאָרֵי הַמִּדּוֹת לְמִדַּת הַהִתְנַשְׂאוּת,
דְּכָל הַמִּדּוֹת מִתְעוֹרְרוֹת גַּם מִדָּבָר שֶׁאֵינָם מֵעֶרְכָּם, וּכְמוֹ
הַבְּהֵמָה רַבָּה שֶׁבְּנִינְוֵה[כט] הִיא טַעַם עַל הָרַחֲמִים.

מַה שֶּׁאֵין כֵּן מִדַּת הַהִתְנַשְׂאוּת הִיא דַּוְקָא עַל יְדֵי הַזּוּלַת
וּמִי שֶׁבְּעֶרְכּוֹ, דִּכְשֶׁיֵּשׁ לָאָדָם אֶלֶף אֲלָפִים בְּהֵמוֹת וְעוֹפוֹת,
לֹא יִתְעוֹרֵר בְּמִדַּת הַהִתְנַשְׂאוּת, כִּי אִם עַל יְדֵי הָאָדָם דַּוְקָא.

---

95. **Jonah, end [4:11].**
The final verse of Jonah contains a rhetorical question asked by G-d of Jonah: *Shall I not feel pity for the great city of Nineveh, in which there are more than a hundred and twenty thousand people who do not know their right hand from their left, and many animals?* The fact that the attribute of mercy can be awakened even by animals, who are certainly not in G-d's or even Jonah's class, demonstrates that the other attributes can be awakened by beings of a different class.

96. The latency of the other attributes can be compared to the latency of the fire of coal, which emerges with ease. Similarly, the other attributes are easi-

ly animated, even by beings that are not on the human level (such as animals). The latency of *malchut*, on the other hand, is compared to the latency of the fire within flint, which requires much effort to extract. Similarly, the attribute of exaltedness is not easily animated, and requires other human beings.

Their states of latency, then, are very different. The other attributes, even in their latency, are "apparent entities," which lend themselves easily to manifestation. The latent state of *malchut*, by contrast, is much more severe; it is a "hidden entity" even in its latency. The attribute of exaltedness is therefore not easily lent to animation.

5.

The above serves as an analogy for the supernal realm.[97] All of the [supernal] attributes[98] are revelations of the blessed Infinite Light. They come into being because of the Infinite Light—not because of the worlds, and not as a response to human instigation.[99]

Although the attributes relate to the worlds—as the verse says, *O G-d, remember Your mercies and Your kindnesses, for they are* me'olam *(eternal)*,[100] implying that mercies and kindnesses relate to the worlds (*olamot*)[101]—this is true only in the sense that the attributes are on a level that *relates* to the worlds.[102] For the levels beyond the attributes[103] do not relate to the worlds, whereas the attributes are on a level that does relate to the worlds. But this does not mean that the attributes are *for* the worlds. Indeed, the attributes are revelations that come into being because of the Infinite Light. It is just that they are also on a level that *relates* to worlds.[104]

THE LOWER SEVEN

By way of illustration, let us consider the fact that the seven lower attributes of each *sefirah* relate to the *sefirah* directly beneath them.[105] This does not mean that they exist *for* the level

---

97. The discourse now applies the distinction drawn between man's emotional attributes and his feeling of exaltedness (*malchut*) to the supernal realm, explaining how the supernal attribute of *malchut* differs from the other attributes.

98. I.e., the six emotive attributes of *chesed* through *yesod* (exclusive of *malchut*); see above, footnote 72.

99. This parallels man's emotional attributes, which, as explained above (end of chapter 3), exist and can become animated irrespective of another being's presence.

100. **Psalms 25:6.**

101. The Hebrew word used in the verse to mean *eternal* is *me'olam* (מעולם). *Olam* (עולם), however, is also the Hebrew word for *world*. In a deeper sense, then, the verse is understood as follows: *O G-d, remember Your mercies and Your kindnesses, for they are* **of the world**—i.e., G-d's attributes (His *mercies and kindnesses*) are of a level that relates to the worlds.

102. Kabbalah and Chasidus explain that Creation occurred through G-d manifesting His attributes. On the

ה.

וְהַדּוּגְמָא מִזֶּה יוּבַן לְמַעְלָה, דְּכָל הַמִּדּוֹת הֵם גִּילּוּיִים מְאוֹר אֵין סוֹף בָּרוּךְ הוּא, וְהַיְינוּ מִצַּד אוֹר אֵין סוֹף, וְלֹא בִּשְׁבִיל הָעוֹלָמוֹת, וְלֹא עַל יְדֵי הִתְעוֹרְרוּת הַתַּחְתּוֹנִים.

וַהֲגַם דְּמִדּוֹת שַׁיָּיכוֹת אֶל הָעוֹלָמוֹת, כְּמוֹ שֶׁכָּתוּב זְכוֹר רַחֲמֶיךָ ה' וַחֲסָדֶיךָ כִּי מֵעוֹלָם הֵמָּה, שֶׁרַחֲמִים וַחֲסָדִים שַׁיָּיכִים אֶל הָעוֹלָמוֹת, הִנֵּה זֶה מַה שֶּׁהַמִּדּוֹת הֵם גַּם כֵּן בְּהַמַּדְרֵיגָה שֶׁשַּׁיָּיכָה אֶל הָעוֹלָמוֹת, דִּבְחִינָה וּמַדְרֵיגָה שֶׁלְּמַעְלָה מֵהַמִּדּוֹת אֵינָן שַׁיָּיכוֹת לָעוֹלָמוֹת, וְהַמִּדּוֹת הֵן בְּמַדְרֵיגָה שֶׁשַּׁיָּיכָה לָעוֹלָמוֹת, אֲבָל לֹא שֶׁהַמִּדּוֹת הֵן בִּשְׁבִיל הָעוֹלָמוֹת, דְּהַמִּדּוֹת הֵם גִּילּוּיִים מִצַּד אוֹר אֵין סוֹף, אֶלָּא שֶׁהֵם גַּם כֵּן בְּאוֹתָהּ הַמַּדְרֵיגָה מַה שֶּׁשַּׁיָּיךְ אֶל הָעוֹלָמוֹת.

וּכְמוֹ בְּזֶ' תַּחְתּוֹנוֹת שֶׁבְּכָל סְפִירָה וּסְפִירָה, שֶׁהֵם שַׁיָּיכִים לְמַדְרֵיגָה שֶׁלְּמַטָּה מִמֶּנָּה, הֲרֵי אֵין זֶה שֶׁהֵם בִּשְׁבִיל הַמַּדְרֵיגָה

---

first day of Creation, G-d manifested His attribute of *chesed*; on the second day, G-d manifested His attribute of *gevurah*; and so on. The Six Days of Creation, then, refer to the manifestation of the six supernal attributes to create the worlds (see *Zohar* cited below, footnote 115). It is thus understood that the supernal attributes are not completely beyond the worlds, transcending Creation, but are rather of a level that can and does relate to the worlds.

103. This refers to the loftier "intellectual" *sefirot* of *chochmah*, *binah* and *daat* (see above, footnote 72), and the spiritual dimensions that transcend the *sefirot*. See *Beshaah She-*

hikdimu 5672, vol. 1, p. 75.

104. Saying that the supernal attributes exist *for* the worlds implies that G-d only manifests His attributes in order to facilitate Creation. This, however, is not the case. The supernal attributes come into being for G-d Himself, because He wishes to be expressed through these various attributes. So although they ultimately do *relate* to the worlds, they are not emanated *for* the worlds.

105. Each of the ten *sefirot* is comprised of ten sub-*sefirot*. *Chesed*, for example, contains within it elements of *chochmah*, *binah*, *daat*, *chesed*, *gevurah*, *tiferet*, *hod*, *yesod* and *malchut*.

beneath them. Rather, they exist within the higher level. It is just that they are also on a level that relates to the lower level, as expressed in the saying, "The external dimension of the higher level becomes the internal dimension of the lower level."[106] But it is not as though the seven lower attributes exist *for* the lower level; for indeed, they complete the *higher* level.[107]

INTELLECT AND EMOTIONS

Take, for example, intellect and emotions. The emotions of the heart come into being from intellectual excitement—the "emotions" of the intellect. But this does not mean that the emotions of the intellect exist *for* the emotions of the heart. Rather, the emotions of the intellect complete the intellect.

[To illustrate this point:] When a person understands and grasps a Divine concept in his mind, he becomes excited in his mind by the goodness of the concept. This excitement, which is the emotional aspect of the intellect, completes the intellect, because it demonstrates that the individual understands and grasps the concept. If he would not understand and grasp it he would not become excited about it. A lack of excitement is a sign of a lack of understanding. So the emotions of the intellect complete the intellect.

The fact that from the emotions of the intellect come the

Now, the seven lower elements of a *sefirah*—i.e., *chesed* through *malchut*—relate to the *sefirah* directly below it. For example, the seven lower elements of *chesed* relate to *gevurah*. The three first elements of a *sefirah*, however—the elements of *chochmah*, *binah* and *daat*—do not relate to the *sefirah* beneath them.

106. See *Eitz Chaim, Shaar* 14, ch. 9; *Likkutei Torah, Shelach,* s.v. *Inyan Hanesachim* [41c].

Likkutei Torah, ibid.: Anything that exists contains an internal dimension and an external dimension. The internal dimension refers to its reception of energy and life-force, as well as its attachment to its antecedent. The external dimension refers to its giving to others.

Every fruit, for example, has two aspects: the taste of the fruit, which is an intangible entity, and the tangible substance of the fruit. Now, within the taste there are two powers: 1) The power to receive its energy from the stars (which are what cause vegetation to grow); 2) the power to bestow its energy and taste into the physical sub-

שֶׁלְּמַטָּה מֵהֶם, אֶלָּא שֶׁהֵם בְּמַדְרֵיגָה הָעֶלְיוֹנָה, אֶלָּא דְּהֵם גַּם
כֵּן בְּמַדְרֵיגָה שֶׁשַּׁיֶּיכָה לְמַדְרֵיגָה תַּחְתּוֹנָה מֵהֶם, וּכְמַאֲמָר
חִיצוֹנִית שֶׁבָּעֶלְיוֹןⁱⁱ נַעֲשָׂה פְּנִימִית אֶל הַתַּחְתּוֹן, אֲבָל אֵין זֶה
שֶׁהֲרֵי׳ תַּחְתּוֹנוֹת הֵם בִּשְׁבִיל הַמַּדְרֵיגָה הַתַּחְתּוֹנָה, שֶׁהֲרֵי הֵם
מַשְׁלִימִים הַמַּדְרֵיגָה הָעֶלְיוֹנָה.

וּכְמוֹ בְּשֵׂכֶל וּמִדּוֹת, הִנֵּה מֵהִתְפַּעֲלוּת הַשֵּׂכֶל, שֶׁהוּא מִדּוֹת
שֶׁבַּשֵּׂכֶל, נַעֲשִׂים הַמִּדּוֹת שֶׁבַּלֵּב, הֲרֵי אֵין זֶה שֶׁהַמִּדּוֹת
שֶׁבַּשֵּׂכֶל הֵם בִּשְׁבִיל הַמִּדּוֹת שֶׁבַּלֵּב, אֶלָּא שֶׁהַמִּדּוֹת שֶׁבַּשֵּׂכֶל
הֵן מַשְׁלִימוֹת הַשֵּׂכֶל.

דְּכַאֲשֶׁר הָאָדָם מֵבִין וּמַשִּׂיג בְּשִׂכְלוֹ הַשָּׂגָה אֱלֹקִית, הֲרֵי
הוּא מִתְפַּעֵל בְּמוֹחוֹ עַל טוּב הַהַשָּׂגָה הַהִיא, הִנֵּה הִתְפַּעֲלוּת
זֹאת שֶׁהִיא הַמִּדּוֹת שֶׁבַּשֵּׂכֶל מַשְׁלִים אֶת הַשֵּׂכֶל, דְּזֶהוּ הוֹרָאָה
שֶׁמֵּבִין וּמַשִּׂיג אֶת הַשֵּׂכֶל, דְּאִם לֹא הָיָה מְבִינוֹ וּמַשִּׂיגוֹ לֹא
הָיָה מִתְפַּעֵל עַל זֶה, דְּהֶעְדֵּר הַהִתְפַּעֲלוּת הוֹרָאָה עַל הֶעְדֵּר
הַהֲבָנָה וְהַשָּׂגָה, הֲרֵי דְּמִדּוֹת שֶׁבַּשֵּׂכֶל הֵם מַשְׁלִימִים אֶת
הַשֵּׂכֶל.

וּמַה שֶּׁמִּדּוֹת שֶׁבַּשֵּׂכֶל נַעֲשִׂים מִדּוֹת שֶׁבַּלֵּב, הוּא לְפִי

---

stance of the fruit. The first is its internal dimension; the second, its external dimension.

The same is true of the soul of man. The internal dimension of the soul cleaves to its source to receive its sustenance, while the external dimension gives life to the body.

And so it is throughout the "chain of existence" (*seder hishtalshelut*): the external dimension of a higher level becomes the internal dimension of the lower level. But the internal dimension of the higher level does not descend to the lower level.

(The internal dimension is called *penimiyut*, from the word *panim*, which connotes *turning*, since the internal dimension turns toward and cleaves to its source. The external dimension is called *chitzoniyut*, from the word *chitzon*, which connotes *outside*, since it bestows its energy to that which is outside it.)

107. Although the seven lower elements of each *sefirah* relate (and transmit energy) to the *sefirah* directly beneath them, they nonetheless do not exist *for* the lower *sefirah*.

emotions of the heart is because the emotions of the intellect are similar in character to the emotions of the heart; for emotions in general [whether of the mind or heart] are characterized by animation and excitement. But this does not mean that the emotions of the intellect exist *for* the emotions of the heart.

In other words, the intellect itself transcends emotions. Only the lower seven elements of the intellect, i.e., the emotions of the intellect, are on the same level—animation and excitement—as the emotions of the heart, and therefore cause the awakening of the emotions of the heart. But this does not mean that they exist *for* the emotions of the heart.

SUPERNAL ATTRIBUTES

And so it is with the supernal attributes. They are revelations from the Infinite Light *because of the Infinite Light*.[108] Although they are on a level that relates to the worlds, they nonetheless do not exist *for* the worlds.[109]

Not so in the case of the attribute of *malchut*. *Malchut* is a revelation from the Infinite Light *for the worlds*[110]; as in the saying, "There is no king without a nation."[111] And it is the creatures of the lower worlds that awaken the desire for [His] kingship, as in the saying, "G-d says: 'Recite before Me… verses of kingship so that you proclaim Me as King over you.'"[112] And the beginning of the awakening of [His] kingship came through Adam, who accepted[113] the kingship of

---

108. I.e., for no other purpose; not for any other need. *Malchut*, as the discourse will soon point out, differs, as it exists *for the worlds*.

109. As mentioned above (footnote 102), the supernal attributes were employed in the creation of the worlds; yet this is not the purpose of their existence. They are an integral part *of* Creation, but are not manifested expressly *for* Creation.

110. *Malchut* differs from the other supernal attributes in that it is emanated exclusively *for the worlds*; its entire purpose is to be a "King" over Creation. Furthermore, as the discourse will soon say, *malchut* is awakened only in *response* to the desire of the created beings to have a King, and is not Self-initiated like the other attributes.

111. *Emek Hamelech, Shaar Shaashu'ei Hamelech*, ch. 1, beg.; *Sefer*

דְּמִדּוֹת שֶׁבַּשֵּׂכֶל הֵם קְרוֹבִים בְּעִנְיָנָם אֶל הַמִּדּוֹת שֶׁבַּלֵּב, דִּכְלָלוּת עִנְיַן הַמִּדּוֹת הוּא עִנְיַן הַהִתְרַגְּשׁוּת וְהַהִתְפַּעֲלוּת, אֲבָל אֵין זֶה שֶׁהַמִּדּוֹת שֶׁבַּשֵּׂכֶל הֵם בִּשְׁבִיל הַמִּדּוֹת שֶׁבַּלֵּב.

וְהַיְינוּ שֶׁהַמּוֹחִין הֵם לְמַעֲלָה מֵעִנְיַן הַמִּדּוֹת, וְרַק הַז' תַּחְתּוֹנוֹת שֶׁבַּמּוֹחִין שֶׁהֵם הַמִּדּוֹת שֶׁבַּשֵּׂכֶל הֵם בְּאוֹתָהּ הַמַּדְרֵיגָה, הַיְינוּ עִנְיַן הַהִתְרַגְּשׁוּת וְהַהִתְפַּעֲלוּת, כְּמוֹ הַמִּדּוֹת שֶׁבַּלֵּב, לָכֵן הֵם הַפּוֹעֲלִים הַתְעוֹרְרוּת הַמִּדּוֹת שֶׁבַּלֵּב, אֲבָל אֵין זֶה שֶׁהֵם בִּשְׁבִיל הַמִּדּוֹת שֶׁבַּלֵּב.

וְכֵן הוּא בְּמִדּוֹת הָעֶלְיוֹנוֹת, שֶׁהֵם גִּילּוּיִים מְאוֹר אֵין סוֹף מִצַּד הָאוֹר אֵין סוֹף, אֶלָּא שֶׁהֵם בְּהַמַּדְרֵיגָה שֶׁשַּׁיָּיכָה אֶל הָעוֹלָמוֹת, אֲבָל לֹא שֶׁהֵם בִּשְׁבִיל הָעוֹלָמוֹת.

מַה שֶׁאֵין כֵּן מִדַּת הַמַּלְכוּת הִיא גִּילּוּי מְאוֹר אֵין סוֹף בִּשְׁבִיל הָעוֹלָמוֹת, וּכְמַאֲמָר אֵין מֶלֶךְ[י] בְּלֹא עָם, וְהַהִתְעוֹרְרוּת עַל עִנְיַן הַמְּלוּכָה בָּא עַל יְדֵי הַתַּחְתּוֹנִים, וּכְמַאֲמָר אָמַר הַקָּדוֹשׁ בָּרוּךְ הוּא[י] אִמְרוּ לְפָנַי כוּ' מַלְכִיּוֹת כְּדֵי שֶׁתַּמְלִיכוּנִי עֲלֵיכֶם, וּתְחִלַּת הַהִתְעוֹרְרוּת הַמְּלוּכָה הָיָה עַל יְדֵי אָדָם

Hachaim, Geulah, ch. 2; *Bachya, Vayeshev*, 38:30; *Tanya*, **Part II** [*Shaar Hayichud Veha'emunah*], **ch. 7.**

112. *Rosh Hashanah* 34b.
Rosh Hashanah ibid.: "Said Rabbah: 'G-d says, 'Recite before Me on Rosh Hashanah verses of kingship, verses of remembrance, and verses of *shofar*. Verses of kingship, so that you proclaim Me as King over you. Verses of remembrance, so that your remembrance may come before Me for good. And with what [is this done]? With the *shofar*.'"
Our Sages thus established a three-fold prayer service for Rosh Hashanah, recited at Musaf, comprised of Biblical verses pertaining to these three subjects: G-d's kingship, G-d remembering His people, and the sounding of the *shofar*.

113. *Pirkei d'Rabbi Eliezer*, ch. 11.
Pirkei d'Rabbi Eliezer, ibid.: "Adam appeared to be a divine being. The creatures looked at Adam and were in awe of him. They thought he was their creator and came to bow before him. Adam said to them, 'Have you come to bow down before *me*? Let I and you go and garb [G-d] with gran-

Heaven, and said, *G-d has reigned....*[114]

So the revelation of the other supernal attributes comes about because of the blessed Infinite Light, as it says, *For six days G-d made the heaven and the earth....*[115] But the revelation of the attribute of *malchut* took place through Adam, since it is a revelation from the Infinite Light *for the worlds.*[116]

NAME

Malchut is therefore called "name."[117] As in the saying, "His name was proclaimed King"[118] over them. For just as the general purpose of a name is for the sake of another person,[119] likewise, the *sefirah* of *malchut* is a revelation that occurs for the sake of the worlds.

Now, although a name exists for the sake of others, the *essence* of the name is for oneself, since it is in it and through it

---

deur and strength, and coronate He who created us. For it is the nation that coronates the king; and if the nation does not coronate the king, the king cannot coronate himself.' At that moment, Adam began coronating G-d, with the other creatures replying after him, saying (Psalms 93:1): *G-d has reigned; He has garbed Himself with grandeur....*"

114. Psalms 93:1.

115. **Exodus 20:11, following the interpretation of the *Zohar* (II:89b) that the *six days* refer to the six attributes** [of *chesed, gevurah, tiferet, netzach, hod* and *yesod*].

The verse does not say, *In six days G-d made...*, but rather, *Six days G-d made....*, implying that G-d lowered the six supernal attributes themselves into the realm of *Asiyah* in order to create the world (*Sefer Hamaamarim 5708*, p. 272; see also above, footnote 102).

116. The six supernal attributes that were employed during the Six Days of Creation were manifest by G-d Himself, without the elicitation of Adam. It was only the attribute of *malchut* that required Adam's elicitation for it to become manifest. This is a clear indication of *malchut's* distinction from the other attributes. Unlike the other attributes, which are Self-initiated, *malchut* can only be awakened by *others*, as its entire existence is *for the worlds.*

The six supernal attributes are thus likened to the fire of coal (mentioned in the previous chapter): they exist as an "apparent entity" on their own—i.e., because of the Infinite Light—irrespective of their role in the creation of the worlds. *Malchut*, by contrast, is likened to the fire of flint: on its own it is a "hidden entity"; it first becomes apparent when it is forcibly extracted by an *outside source.*

What is the reason for this distinction? The other attributes are designed to complement and define

הָרִאשׁוֹן, שֶׁקִּבֵּל[117] מַלְכוּת שָׁמַיִם וְאָמַר ה' מָלָךְ וְגו'.

דְּהִתְגַּלּוּת הַמִּדּוֹת הָעֶלְיוֹנוֹת הֵם מִצַּד אוֹר אֵין סוֹף בָּרוּךְ הוּא, וּכְמוֹ שֶׁכָּתוּב כִּי שֵׁשֶׁת[115] יָמִים עָשָׂה ה' אֶת הַשָּׁמַיִם וְאֶת הָאָרֶץ, אֲבָל הִתְגַּלּוּת בְּחִינַת הַמְּלוּכָה הָיָה עַל יְדֵי אָדָם הָרִאשׁוֹן, לְפִי שֶׁמִּדַּת הַמַּלְכוּת הִיא גִּילּוּי מְאוֹר אֵין סוֹף בִּשְׁבִיל הָעוֹלָמוֹת.

וְלָכֵן נִקְרֵאת סְפִירַת הַמַּלְכוּת בְּתוֹאַר שֵׁם, וּכְמַאֲמָר מֶלֶךְ שְׁמוֹ[118] נִקְרָא עֲלֵיהֶם, דְּכְשֵׁם שֶׁכְּלָלוּת עִנְיַן הַשֵּׁם הוּא בִּשְׁבִיל הַזּוּלַת, הִנֵּה כֵּן הוּא בִּסְפִירַת הַמַּלְכוּת, שֶׁהוּא גִּילּוּי שֶׁהוּא בִּשְׁבִיל הָעוֹלָמוֹת.

וְעִם הֱיוֹת דְּהַשֵּׁם הוּא בִּשְׁבִיל הַזּוּלַת, הִנֵּה עֶצֶם הַשֵּׁם הוּא

one's "self"—in the human example, one is complemented and defined by his kindness, his compassion, etc. *Malchut*, however, means to be higher than *something else*—someone *outside* oneself. Therefore, *malchut* comes into being only when there are others over which to be "king," and only when they actively (forcefully) elicit this attribute.

117. *Pardes, Shaar Erchei Hakinuyim, Maarechet Shem.*

118. **From the hymn** *Adon Olam.*

119. A name exists only for the sake of others. One who is alone on an island does not need a name. A name is only necessary so that one can be differentiated from others and identified. *Malchut* is therefore called "name," since it too exists only in the presence, and for the sake, of others.

Likkutei Torah, Behar, 41c states:

"The light of the sun, for example, which shines upon the earth and its inhabitants, is considered as naught in comparison to the essence of the sun, which is the source of its light and radiance. There is no difference to the sun whether its light shines upon the earth or if it is blocked by clouds or window shades—this has no affect on the sun itself.

"The same is true of the Infinite Light. It is only a ray that emanates from Him. Through many contractions, this light becomes perceptible to the 'holy ones' [the angels]. This light is also called 'name.' Such appellations are meant to help us understand the nature of the Divine energy that gives life to the worlds—how it does not affect the Essence of G-d at all. For this is true of a given name, such as Abraham: The name is not comparable at all to the essence of the person, and does not affect him at all, since he does not need the name for himself."

that vitality flows and is revealed.[120] The same is true of the *sefirah* of *malchut*—it is in it and through it that the worlds are created and given life.[121]

And although the general creation and flow of vitality [to the worlds] is channeled through the *sefirah* of *malchut*, nevertheless, the *sefirah* of *malchut* is referred to by the appellation "name" since it is a revelation that occurs for the sake of the worlds.[122]

---

120. See **Likkutei Torah**, s.v. **Et Shabtotai**, ch. 2 [*Behar* 41c]; **below, discourse entitled Be'etzem Hayom** [*Sefer Hamaamarim 5701*, p. 82].

The Hebrew name of a person, for example, is the conduit through which the energy and life-force of the soul is channeled to the body. See below.

From *Likkutei Torah*, ibid.: "The life-force of a being is vested within the letters of its name. As Scripture states regarding Adam (Genesis 2:19), *[G-d] brought [every creature] to Adam, to see what he would call each one; and whatever Adam called each living creature, that remained its name.* (Adam

was able to perceive the distinct Divine energy that was vested in each animal, and so named them.) There is a real connection between a thing and its name; it is not just an arbitrary appellation. As it says in *Shaar Hayichud Veha'emunah*, ch. 1, end, 'The name by which [the creature] is called in the Holy Tongue is a vessel for the life-force condensed into the letters of that name, which has descended from the 'ten utterances'....' Similarly, before the soul of man enters the body, it does not have a name at all (see *Ramban* on Genesis 2:20). So the name is not for the soul itself, nor does it achieve anything for the body.

בִּשְׁבִיל עַצְמוֹ, שֶׁבּוֹ וְעַל יָדוֹ[י] הוּא הַמְשָׁכַת וְגִילּוּי הַחַיּוּת, הִנֵּה כֵן הוּא בִּסְפִירַת הַמַּלְכוּת שֶׁבָּהּ וְעַל יָדָהּ הוּא הִתְהַוּוּת הָעוֹלָמוֹת וְחַיּוּתָן.

וְעִם הֱיוֹת דְּכִלְלוּת הַהִתְהַוּוּת וְהַמְשָׁכַת הַחַיּוּת הוּא עַל יְדֵי סְפִירַת הַמַּלְכוּת, הִנֵּה סְפִירַת הַמַּלְכוּת נִקְרָא בְּתוֹאַר שֵׁם, שֶׁהוּא גִּילּוּי שֶׁבִּשְׁבִיל הָעוֹלָמוֹת.

Rather, the name binds the soul to the body, and the life-force that comes forth from the soul and gives life to the body is rooted in the name...."

121. Just as a name is the conduit of life and vitality for the body, similarly, the attribute of *malchut* is the conduit of life and vitality for the worlds (as mentioned above, ch. 3).

122. I.e., although *malchut* is a primary channel of vitality, the energy channeled through it is *for the worlds*. This further underscores how *malchut* exists entirely for the sake of Creation.

The discourse has thus established the uniqueness of the *sefirah* of *malchut*, in that unlike the other supernal attributes, *malchut* exists solely for the sake of the worlds, or more specifically, for the sake of creating and vivifying the worlds. *Malchut*, then, can be seen as the *sefirah* furthest from G-d's Essence, as it is the one that actualizes the creation of "independent," limited worlds.

In the following chapter, the discourse will examine various dimensions of *malchut*, ultimately concluding that it is the lowest dimension of *malchut*, mere Divine "radiance," that actually effects Creation.

6.

The explanation of the matter is as follows: The fact that *malchut* is called "name" refers to the general concept of the attribute of *malchut*, even as it exists within *Atzilut*.[123] This is because *malchut* in general [even as it exists in *Atzilut*] is revelation, i.e., a revelation to the worlds.[124]

For it is known that the attribute of *malchut* within each *sefirah* is the "actuality" and "self" of that *sefirah*—i.e., it is the particular revelation of that *sefirah*.[125]

DIFFERENT TYPES OF KINDNESS

[To explain]: Every revelation and awakening emerges at first in a general way and later in a specific and measured form.

Take, for example, the attribute of kindness. At first, there is an awakening to bestow kindness. But this awakening is still a general one; it is [as of yet] not at all apparent which *type* of kindness it will be. For there are different types of kindnesses: there is physical kindness and there is spiritual kindness, e.g., teaching an idea to someone or helping someone acquire good character traits.

There are also various methods of bestowing kindness. One can bestow kindness with one's money alone, or also with one's body, or with one's soul as well, as mentioned in *Orchot Tzadikim*[126] regarding Abraham our forefather, who bestowed kindness with his money, body and soul.[127]

---

123. ATZILUT. Kabbalah and Chasidus speak of four supernal worlds. Of these, *Atzilut* is the loftiest. It is a G-dly world (*Tanya*, ch. 49). In *Atzilut*, there is no feeling of self or being, just an awareness of something higher, something beyond—G-dliness. *Atzilut* is therefore not considered to be a *created* world, but rather an *emanated* world. It is in *Atzilut* that G-d's attributes (the ten *sefirot*) are first manifest. There, however, the attributes are in a much loftier—infinite—state. For more on *Atzilut*, see *The Four Worlds*

(Kehot, 2003).

124. As *malchut* resides within the G-dly world of *Atzilut*, it cannot be spoken of as existing *for* the lower worlds. Yet, of all of the other attributes, *malchut* is the one most closely connected with the lower worlds, as it is "a revelation *to* the worlds."

125. See **Likkutei Torah, biur on Eileh Masei (the third discourse by that title)** [92b]:

"The seventh level of each attribute

ו.

וּבֵיאוּר הָעִנְיָן הוּא, דְּהִנֵּה זֶה מַה שֶׁהַמַּלְכוּת נִקְרָא שֵׁם הוּא בִּכְלָלוּת מִדַּת הַמַּלְכוּת גַּם כְּמוֹ שֶׁהִיא בַּאֲצִילוּת, מִפְּנֵי שֶׁהַמַּלְכוּת בִּכְלָל הִיא גִּילּוּי, הַיְינוּ גִּילּוּי אֶל הָעוֹלָמוֹת.

דִּכְשֵׁם שֶׁמִּדַּת הַמַּלְכוּת בְּכָל סְפִירָה הֲרֵי יָדוּעַ שֶׁזֶּהוּ⁷ֿ¹ הַמְּצִיאוּת וְהַיֵּשׁוּת שֶׁבְּהַסְּפִירָה, וְהַיְינוּ דְּזֶהוּ הַגִּילּוּי פְּרָטִי שֶׁל הַסְּפִירָה.

דְּהִנֵּה כָּל גִּילּוּי וְהִתְעוֹרְרוּת, הִנֵּה בַּתְּחִלָּה הוּא בָּא בְּאוֹפֶן כְּלָלִי וְאַחֲרֵי כֵן בְּאוֹפֶן פְּרָטִי וּמָדוּד.

וּכְמוֹ מִדַּת הַחֶסֶד, הֲרֵי תְּחִלָּה הוּא הַהִתְעוֹרְרוּת לְהֵטִיב חַסְדּוֹ, אֲבָל הִתְעוֹרְרוּת זוֹ הִיא כְּלָלִית עֲדַיִין, וְאֵינוֹ נִיכָּר כְּלָל בַּמֶּה יְהֵא חַסְדּוֹ. כִּי בְּחֶסֶד יֵשׁ כַּמָּה סוּגֵי חֶסֶד, יֵשׁ חֶסֶד גַּשְׁמִי וְיֵשׁ חֶסֶד רוּחָנִי בְּהַשְׁפָּעַת הַשֵּׂכֶל וְקִנְיַן מִדּוֹת טוֹבוֹת.

וְיֵשׁ כַּמָּה אוֹפַנִּים בְּאוֹפַנֵּי הַשְׁפָּעַת הַחֶסֶד, אִם רַק בְּמָמוֹנוֹ אוֹ גַּם בְּגוּפוֹ אוֹ גַּם בְּנַפְשׁוֹ, וְכִדְאִיתָא בְּאָרְחוֹת צַדִּיקִים בְּאַבְרָהָם אָבִינוּ עָלָיו הַשָּׁלוֹם, שֶׁהָיָה נָדִיב בְּמָמוֹנוֹ בְּגוּפוֹ וּבְנַפְשׁוֹ.

[i.e., the level of *malchut* within each attribute] is the revelation of that particular attribute... the 'actuality' of that attribute.... During the counting of the *omer* [see below, footnote 131], we count seven levels within each of the seven attributes, for the main purpose of the counting is that there be a revelation and flow 'downward'—which is the function of the seventh level of each attribute, the revelation of that particular attribute."

126. Beginning of ch. 17.

127. Abraham was known for his ex-

traordinary generosity and hospitality (see *Sotah* 10a—cited below, footnote 228). Not only did he give of his money, providing expensive delicacies to all of his guests, he gave of his body as well, standing over the guests and personally tending to their needs. Even while recovering from his circumcision, he *ran* to prepare food for his guests (Genesis 18:7). Furthermore, he gave of his soul, dedicating his life to explaining Monotheism to the pagans around him (see *Sefer Hamaamarim 5698*, p. 129; below, ch. 9).

GENERAL AND PARTICULAR

So when the general awakening [to bestow kindness] occurs, it is not yet apparent which type of kindness it will be and with which method it will be bestowed—it is just a general awakening.

After this general awakening, a specific awakening follows in which the type and method of the kindness is decided.

Yet even this awakening is [relatively] general, and only later develops in a more specific way, in a way that it is measured specifically according to the level of the recipient. This is [what is termed] a specific and measured revelation.[128]

This revelation, as it occurs in the supernal attributes, occurs in the *sefirah* of *malchut*; for *malchut* is a specific revelation that conforms to the level of the recipient.[129]

FORTY-TWO & FORTY-NINE

This is the general difference between the travels [of the Israelites in the desert][130] and the counting[131] of the *omer*.[132]

---

128. I.e., this is a revelation that is not general or abstract, but specific and measured.

129. MALCHUT=REVELATION. When kindness is initially awakened in a person, it can result in immense giving or in manners that the recipient cannot receive at all. This is because of the undefined nature of the kindness prior to its concretization. Because it still nebulous, it can be infinite and multidimensional.

This is an analogy for the status of *chesed* in *Atzilut*: undefined, infinite and incapable of operating in the lower worlds (*Beriah, Yetzirah* and *Asiyah*). The same is true of all the *sefirot* as they exist in *Atzilut*.

Furthermore, as they exist in *Atzilut*, they are in a state of ascent, cleaving to and enveloping themselves in the Infinite Light, the Emanator.

They are in a state of self-nullification, which is a prerequisite for reception, since if one is processing while receiving he will not receive properly. They therefore do not pass on their energy to the next level—"since they are occupied with absorbing they do not emit."

Malchut, however, is the level of revelation—revealing all that is hidden. It is therefore called *alma d'itgalya*—the revealed world—and speech, since in speech one reveals the secrets of the heart to another. "The spirit of *adam* (man, *mah, z'a*—the six *sefirot*) is to ascend; the spirit of *behema* (animal, *ban—malchut*) is to descend."

This is *malchut*'s function as a subdivision of each *sefirah*. Each *sefirah*, without the element of *malchut*, is in a state of non-being and ascent. *Malchut* provides the *sefirah* with con-

הִנֵּה בְּהַהִתְעוֹרְרוּת כְּלָלִית הֲרֵי אֵינוֹ נִיכָּר עֲדַיִין בְּאֵיזֶה סוּג חֶסֶד יִהְיֶה וּבְאֵיזֶה אוֹפֶן, וְהוּא רַק הִתְעוֹרְרוּת כְּלָלִית בִּלְבָד.

וְאַחֲרֵי הַהִתְעוֹרְרוּת כְּלָלִית הִנֵּה בָּא הִתְעוֹרְרוּת פְּרָטִית, דִּבְהִתְעוֹרְרוּת זוֹ הֲרֵי נֶחְלָט סוּג הַחֶסֶד וְאוֹפַנּוּ.

אֲבָל גַּם הִתְעוֹרְרוּת זוֹ הִיא כְּלָלִית עֲדַיִין, וּבָא אַחֲרֵי כֵן בְּדֶרֶךְ פְּרָט בִּמְדִידָה פְּרָטִית לְפִי עֵרֶךְ הַמְקַבֵּל, שֶׁהוּא גִילוּי פְּרָטִי וּמָדוּד.

הִנֵּה גִילוּי זֶה בְּמִדּוֹת הָעֶלְיוֹנוֹת הוּא בִּסְפִירַת הַמַּלְכוּת, לִהְיוֹתוֹ גִילוּי פְּרָטִי לְפִי עֵרֶךְ הַמְקַבֵּל.

שֶׁזֶּהוּ כְּלָלוּתוֹ^{לט} הַהֶפְרֵשׁ בֵּין הַמַּסָּעוֹת לִסְפִירַת הָעוֹמֶר.

---

creteness and the power of descent and revelation.

Chochmah of *Atzilut*, for example, is in a state of absolute self-nullification and ascent. *Malchut* of *chochmah* reveals *chochmah* by making it into a "something" so that it can then become a source for *chochmah* of *Beriah*. When it becomes *chochmah* of *Beriah* it is then something that the souls and angels can comprehend and thereby perceive Divinity. But as it exists in *Atzilut* it cannot provide any intellectual understanding of Divinity to the worlds, since it is far beyond the understanding of the creatures. Only through *malchut* of *chochmah* can it descend. The same is true of *chesed*: through *malchut* of *chesed* the creatures of the lower worlds are able to achieve a love and ecstatic yearning for the Divine. So *malchut* is the revelation and expansion of each *sefirah* (*Sefer Hamaamarim 5687*, p. 21 ff.).

130. The Israelites journey from Egypt to the Land of Israel was com-

prised of forty-two segments (see Numbers 33:1). This is referred to as the "forty-two travels."

131. COUNTING OF THE OMER. See Leviticus 23:9-16. The *omer* was an offering brought in the *Beit Hamikdash* on the second day of Pesach, containing a specified measure of the first barley harvest of the year. From the time the *omer* was offered and until the festival of Shavuot, a span of forty-nine days, there was a commandment to count each day, making a mention of its relationship to when the *omer* offering was brought. For example, on the first day one would count: "Today is one day of the *omer*." On the seventh day: "Today is seven days, which is one week of the *omer*." Even today, although we cannot bring the *omer* offering as there is no *Beit Hamikdash*, we still perform the mitzvah of the counting of the *omer*.

132. See *Likkutei Torah*, ibid.
Both the forty-two travels of the

The number of travels [from Egypt to the Holy Land] equaled forty-two, which is 7x6—*six* being [representative of] the six attributes. The [seventh] *sefirah, malchut,* is not counted. The number of days of the counting of the *omer,* by contrast, is forty-nine, which is 7x7—*seven* being [representative of] the seven *sefirot* [i.e., including *malchut*].

This is because the travels were an elevation from below to above,[133] which is why *malchut* is not counted.[134] In the counting of the *omer,* however, which is a flow and revelation [from above] to below,[135] the *sefirah* of *malchut* is counted.

INHERENT EXALTEDNESS

Now, because revelation takes place through *malchut,* it is called "name," which is a revelation to others.

And although the fact that *malchut* is called "name" refers to *malchut* in general, even as it exists in *Atzilut,*[136] nevertheless, *malchut,* as it exists in *Atzilut,* is in a state of *in-*

Israelites in the desert and the forty-nine days of the counting of the *omer* are symbolic of the supernal attributes, as will be explained shortly.

The 42 travels correspond to the 42 words in the prayer *Ana Bechoach,* which allude to the seven supernal attributes as they are each comprised of the first six attributes. The prayer therefore contains seven verses, each of contains only six words, since the seventh *sefirah* [i.e., *malchut*] of each attribute is not included in the calculation of the Divine name that equals 42. In the counting of the *omer,* however, there are 49 days; each of the seven attributes is comprised of seven since the *sefirah* of *malchut* is counted as well. Why the discrepancy?

The explanation is as follows: *Malchut* is a "bridge" [connecting a high-

er level with the level below it]. Upon its descent, *malchut* of *Atzilut* becomes *atik* (the "crown") of *Beriah, malchut* of *Beriah* becomes *atik* of *Yetzirah*… and *malchut* of *Ein Sof* becomes *atik* of *Atzilut.* Only the attribute of *malchut* of the higher level descends to become the *atik* and source of the next level.

Now the Divine name that equals 42 represents elevations from below to above…. The seven attributes of that name are therefore comprised of only six attributes, which contain the essence of the given attribute and are the ones that are elevated. But the seventh aspect of each attribute, which is the *revelation* of the attribute [i.e., how the attribute relates to that which is *below* itself, does not ascend]….

The counting of the *omer,* however,

דְּהַמַּסָעוֹת מִסְפָּרָן מ״ב, ז׳ פְּעָמִים ו׳, שֶׁהֵן הַשִּׁשָּׁה מִדּוֹת,
וּסְפִירַת הַמַּלְכוּת אֵינָהּ נֶחְשֶׁבֶת, וּסְפִירַת הָעוֹמֶר מִסְפָּרָן מ״ט,
ז׳ פְּעָמִים ז׳, שֶׁהֵן ז׳ סְפִירוֹת.

וְטַעַם הַדָּבָר הוּא, לְפִי שֶׁהַמַּסָעוֹת הֵם הַעֲלָאָה מִלְּמַטָּה
לְמַעְלָה, וְאֵינוֹ חוֹשֵׁב סְפִירַת הַמַּלְכוּת, וּסְפִירַת הָעוֹמֶר שֶׁהוּא
הַמְשָׁכָה וְגִלּוּי לְמַטָּה חָשִׁיב סְפִירַת הַמַּלְכוּת.

וְלִהְיוֹת הַגִּלּוּי הוּא עַל יְדֵי סְפִירַת הַמַּלְכוּת, לָכֵן הִנֵּה
הַמַּלְכוּת נִקְרֵאת שֵׁם שֶׁהוּא גִּלּוּי אֶל הַזּוּלַת.

וְעִם הֱיוֹת שֶׁזֶּה מַה שֶּׁסְּפִירַת הַמַּלְכוּת נִקְרֵאת שֵׁם הוּא
בִּכְלָלוּת סְפִירַת הַמַּלְכוּת גַּם כְּמוֹ שֶׁהִיא בַּאֲצִילוּת, מִכָּל
מָקוֹם הִנֵּה סְפִירַת הַמַּלְכוּת כְּמוֹ שֶׁהִיא בַּאֲצִילוּת הִיא

---

constitutes *eliciting* energies, *Today is one day,* etc.—*day* meaning radiance and revelation—from *Atzilut* to *Beriah* and from *Beriah* to *Yetzirah* and from *Yetzirah* to *Asiyah,* until it is drawn into the soul of man. We therefore count seven levels within each of the seven attributes, for the main purpose of the counting is that there be a revelation and flow "downward"—which is the function of the seventh level of each attribute [i.e., *malchut*], the revelation of that particular attribute (*Likkutei Torah,* ibid.).

133. The journey from Egypt to the Holy Land represents one's ascent from the lowest depths to the ultimate spiritual heights, "an elevation from below to above."

134. The function of *malchut* is not to elevate, but rather to elicit and ap-

ply the higher levels to a lower sphere. It is therefore not present in the travels, whose purpose was elevation, not application.

135. As mentioned above (footnote 132), the purpose of the counting of the *omer* is to elicit upon oneself the Divine revelation associated with that particular day (*chesed* of *chesed* on the first day, *gevurah* of *chesed* on the second day, etc.). We therefore include *malchut* in this counting, since *malchut* is necessary for revelation.

136. As explained above, *malchut,* on every level, is the specific aspect that signifies revelation. Even as it exist in *Atzilut,* then, *malchut* is synonymous with the concept of a "name," since a name, too, is that aspect that signifies revelation.

herent exaltedness.[137] As in the phrase, "[Lord of the universe] who reigned before anything was created."[138]

For supernal kingship is not like terrestrial kingship. In the terrestrial realm, the nation chooses the king, coronates him, and thereby awakens within him the attribute of kingship, which is the power of exaltedness. As explained above, this awakening must be instigated by others and the others must be other humans. But in the supernal realm, the concept of the *sefirah* of *malchut* [exaltedness] existed before the worlds were created.[139]

The concept of exaltedness over the worlds is the fact that *malchut* pierces through the "curtain"[140] that is between *Atzilut* and [the three lower worlds of] *Beriah, Yetzirah, Asiyah,* and becomes *atik*[141] of *Beriah.*[142]

---

137. *Hitnasut Atzmi*, in the Hebrew.

All of creation is governed by "relativity." Every element exists, in one sense or another, relative to something else. Take a person's emotional attributes, for example. *Chesed*, or giving, exists only in contrast to *gevurah*, witholding. One's giving is recognized as such only because there are times when he does *not* give. But both *chesed* and *gevurah* exist within the person himself; i.e., their relativity is to each other, within the same being.

Malchut, however, is different, for it is relative to elements *outside* of the person. *Malchut*, exaltedness, exists only relative to someone else who is lower, less exalted. One cannot be *high* unless another is *low*. One can be kind without being "kinder than"; one cannot be high without being "higher than."

G-d, however, is not subject to the laws of creation. G-d is Absolute, not relative. Similarly, G-d's attributes are absolute attributes, not relative to each other or anything else. So His attribute of *malchut* is *absolute* high, *pure* high—not "higher than." This is the meaning of *hitnasut atzmi*: inherent, absolute exaltedness.

138. **From the hymn *Adon Olam*.**

139. We seem to have two conflicting notions: On the one hand we say that "There is no king without a nation." On the other hand we say that it is through *malchut* that the world was created. But how could *malchut* have existed prior to the creation of the world and a nation? The answer is that we know that there is a phenomenon known as *malchut* of *Atzilut*, i.e., that G-d is called our King and that through His exalting Himself over us, as it were, to be our King—this exaltedness vivifies and creates us *ex nihilo* and makes us into a nation. But we have no concept of what this "exaltedness" is—though we know its effect—for it is certainly not anything like human exaltedness and kingship, since in the human

בִּבְחִינַת הַתְנַשְּׂאוּת עַצְמִי, וּכְמַאֲמַר אֲשֶׁר מָלַךְ[ם] בְּטֶרֶם כָּל יְצוּר נִבְרָא.

דְּעִנְיַן הַמְּלוּכָה לְמַעְלָה אֵינָהּ דּוֹמָה לִמְלוּכָה לְמַטָּה, דִּמְלוּכָה לְמַטָּה הִנֵּה הָעָם בּוֹחֲרִים בְּהַמֶּלֶךְ וּמַכְתִּירִין אוֹתוֹ, אֲשֶׁר בָּזֶה מְעוֹרְרִים בּוֹ מִדַּת הַמְּלוּכָה שֶׁהוּא כֹּחַ הַהִתְנַשְּׂאוּת, וְכַנִּזְכָּר לְעֵיל שֶׁהַהִתְעוֹרְרוּת הִיא מֵהַזּוּלַת וּמֵאָדָם דַּוְקָא, אֲבָל לְמַעְלָה עִנְיַן סְפִירַת הַמַּלְכוּת הוּא קוֹדֶם שֶׁנִּתְהַוּוּ הָעוֹלָמוֹת.

וְעִנְיַן הַהִתְנַשְּׂאוּת עַל הָעוֹלָמוֹת הוּא מַה שֶּׁבְּחִינַת מַלְכוּת בּוֹקַעַת[מא] אֶת הַפַּרְסָא שֶׁבֵּין אֲצִילוּת לִבְרִיאָה-יְצִירָה-עֲשִׂיָּה, וְנַעֲשֵׂית עַתִּיק לִבְרִיאָה.

---

realm the fact of being a king does not bring subjects into existence (*Derech Mitzvotecha* 175a).

140. PRASSA, in the Hebrew; see *Onkelos* on Exodus 26:36. Between *Atzilut* and *Beriah* (and likewise between the other worlds), there is a *prassa* (curtain) curtailing the higher world, which needs to be "pierced" in order for the light and vitality of the higher world to penetrate and descend to the lower world. See *Eitz Chaim* 42:4 (ibid., ch. 13 ff. of *Klalut ABYA-1*); 44:1; *Iggeret Hakodesh*, 20 (*Tanya* 131b. Bi-Lingual Edition, p. 507); *Mystical Concepts in Chassidism*, chapter 4 (*Worlds*), section 2.

141. The term *atik* denotes the highest level within a given realm. Specifically, *atik* refers to a level that is so high it is considered to be completely beyond the levels beneath it. Hence, the word *atik* is related to the word *ne'etak*, which means "removed from" (see *Torat Chaim, Shemot*, 142b

(Kehot, 2003); *Derech Mitzvotecha* 110b).

When the Kabbalists speak of *malchut* piercing through the curtain that is between *Atzilut* and the lower worlds to become *atik* of *Beriah*, they are indicating two things: Firstly, that *malchut* of *Atzilut* creates the worlds, forming the "beginning" of *Beriah* (for before *malchut's* descent there are no worlds to speak of). Secondly, that even as *malchut* creates, it remains in a state of *atik*, completely beyond and "removed from" the world of *Beriah* (see *Derech Mitzvotecha* 120b).

So even after the worlds come into being through *malchut*, *malchut* retains its quality of exaltedness, remaining completely beyond the worlds. See *Sefer Hamaamarim 5657*, p. 185.

See also following footnote.

142. *Eitz Chaim, Sha'ar Seder a.b.y.a.,* beginning of chapter 6, and *Shaar Derushei ABYA,* chapter 1; *Mishnat Chasidim, Masechet Ha-*

Of this level it is said, *For His name is sublimely transcendent, it is unto Himself*[143]: even His *name* [i.e., *malchut*] is transcendent and exalted over the worlds.[144]

This is the significance of "His name was proclaimed King" over them: [*malchut* relates to the worlds] only in a transcendent manner.[145] This is similar to the name of a king, which spreads out over the country; its presence exists only in a transcendent sense. The *laws* of the country are what control the country in an immanent sense, whereas the name [of the king] is only transcendent.[146] *For His name is sublimely transcendent*—it is exalted and transcendent; and only *its radiance is upon the earth and heavens*.[147]

Earth and heavens in this context refer to upper Gan Eden and lower Gan Eden,[148] [within which shines] only the radiance of the [Divine] splendor. And even this [radiance] pro-

---

briah, **end of chapter 1 and beginning of chapter 2, et al.**

Malchut, as explained above, is defined as revelation; i.e., that which is transmitted to another entity. This is true of *malchut* as it exists on all levels—even when speaking of *malchut* of *Atzilut*. Yet *malchut* of *Atzilut* is unique in that it possesses another trait—*inherent exaltedness*. This means that although *malchut* is expressed as revelation (to the worlds), this revelation is defined by what it is at its essence—inherent exaltedness. So even as *malchut* pierces through the "curtain" between *Atzilut* and the lower worlds of *Beriah, Yetzirah* and *Asiyah*, it does not enter the worlds internally, for it is inherently exalted, completely beyond the worlds. Rather, it becomes *atik* of *Beriah*—a level that although relates to *Beriah* nonetheless *transcends* it, like a crown that remains above the head. (Only later, as *malchut* becomes expressed in letters and words, does it relate to the worlds in an internal

manner, as will be explained below.)

143. **Psalms 148:13.**

144. Even *malchut*, which is the one *sefirah* that represents revelation to the worlds, remains *transcendent*, beyond the worlds.

145. The very same phrase that was used before (end of ch. 5) to indicate that *malchut* is referred to as "name," implying revelation, also indicates that this revelation remains in a state of transcendence "over them" (the worlds)—just as the name of a king "transcends" his subjects (see following footnote).

146. Both the king's laws and his exalted name, or reputation, serve to rule the nation, albeit in different manners. The laws tell the people *what* to do; the name tells them *why* they should do it.

The king's laws are very practical and down-to-earth: governing the

דְּעַל זֶה נֶאֱמַר כִּי נִשְׂגָּב[147] שְׁמוֹ לְבַדּוֹ, דְּגַם בְּחִינַת שְׁמוֹ הוּא נִשְׂגָּב וּמְרוֹמָם מִן הָעוֹלָמוֹת.

וְזֶהוּ מֶלֶךְ שְׁמוֹ נִקְרָא עֲלֵיהֶם, בִּבְחִינַת מַקִּיף לְבַד. וּכְמוֹ שֵׁם הַמֶּלֶךְ שֶׁמִּתְפַּשֵּׁט עַל הַמְּדִינָה, הֲרֵי זֶה רַק בִּבְחִינַת מַקִּיף, דְּחוּקֵּי הַמְּדִינָה הֵם הַהַנְהָגָה הַפְּנִימִית, אֲבָל הַשֵּׁם הוּא מַקִּיף בִּלְבַד, וּבְחִינַת כִּי נִשְׂגָּב שְׁמוֹ, שֶׁהוּא מְרוֹמָם וְנִשְׂגָּב, וְרַק הוֹדוֹ עַל אֶרֶץ וְשָׁמָיִם.

דְּאֶרֶץ וְשָׁמַיִם הֵם גַּן עֵדֶן הָעֶלְיוֹן וְגַן עֵדֶן הַתַּחְתּוֹן[148], שֶׁזֶּהוּ רַק הֶאָרַת הַזִּיו הַזֶּה בִּלְבַד, וְגַם זֶה הוּא תַּעֲנוּג נִפְלָא עַד אֵין קֵץ,

---

people's day-to-day life, decreeing what they can and cannot do, establishing courts, levying taxes, etc. They are therefore "internal" or "immanent," in the sense that they are easily understood and grasped by the people who obey them. Indeed, the laws *must* be understood by the people, for their purpose is that they be fulfilled by the people.

The king's name, however, serves a different, and arguably more vital, function. The function of his name is to remain *above* the people—not to be grasped or understood by the people. It is this very aloofness that sets the tone for his dominion. The very fact that he is so distant from the people instills a strong degree of fear, awe and respect within them, which in turn fuels their subservience to him. All of this occurs precisely because the king's name is aloof, transcending the people. The very aloofness of his name sets the king apart from his nation, setting the stage for their respect and subservience.

There are thus three elements in our analogy: The king himself, who completely transcends his people; the name of the king, which *transmits to the nation* his *transcendence*; and the edicts of the king, which by being understandable—*immanent*—govern the practicalities of daily life.

The same is true above, when speaking of *malchut* of *Atzilut*. Here there are also three levels (the last of which will be explained shortly): *Malchut* in essence, as it is inherently exalted; *malchut* as a "name," transmitting transcendent Divine energy to the worlds; *malchut* as letters of speech, transmitting immanent Divine energy to the worlds. See *Sefer Hamaamarim 5657*, p. 180 ff.

147. Psalms ibid. The essence of *malchut* of *Atzilut* is exalted and transcendent (even as it begins relating to the worlds), since it is of the level of *inherent exaltedness*. Only a *reflection* of *malchut*—its *radiance*—is actually invested within Creation.

148. *Likkutei Torah, Bamidbar,* **end of the *biur* on *Beshaah Shehikdimu* [15b].**

vides wondrous [spiritual] pleasure without end, since it is radiance from the level of His name.[149] Yet it is only splendor
and radiance.[150]

What invests itself in the worlds internally to give them
life is only the letters of speech of *malchut*.[151] As the verse says,
By the word of G-d the heavens were made.[152] It says further, *You*
(attah) *give life to them all*,[153] which refers to the letters from
alef to *tav*.[154] They [the letters] reveal only an external ray [of
Divinity], and even this undergoes *tzimtzum* after *tzimtzum*,
as it says, *They will declare the glory of Your kingdom* (malchut)*,
and tell of Your strength*[155]—*strength* in this context referring to
the level of *gevurot* and *tzimtzum*.[156] And because of this the
worlds came into being as actual and self-aware beings.[157]

---

149. Although the spiritual manifestation in upper and lower Gan
Eden (Paradise) is a mere reflection of
the transcendence of *malchut*, it is still
powerful enough to provide wondrous, limitless spiritual pleasure to
the souls who inhabit these levels.

150. I.e., not the essence of G-d's
"name" (*malchut*).

151. See *Shaar Hayichud Veha'emunah*, ch. 1 (cited above, ch. 2, and
footnote 41; below, Appendix I). See
also above, footnote 68.

    As it is transmitted to the worlds,
malchut of *Atzilut* is divided into two
levels. The first is transcendent over
the worlds, like a king's transcendent
presence in his country, which is embodied in his name. The radiance of

this level is what is enjoyed in both
levels of Gan Eden.

    The second level of *malchut* per-
vades the worlds internally, like the
king's laws, which represent the
king's immanent presence throughout
his country. These are the letters of
Divine speech that bring the worlds
into being after much contraction of
its light.

152. **Psalms 33:6.**

153. **Nehemiah 9:6.**

154. The Hebrew word *attah* (אתה)—
of the verse, *You* (attah*) give life to
them all*—contains the first and last
letters of the *alef-bet*: *alef* (א) and *tav*
(ת). The verse is thus interpreted as
follows: *The letters of the* alef-bet—alef

לִהְיוֹת שֶׁזֶּה הָאָרָה מִבְּחִינַת שְׁמוֹ יִתְבָּרֵךְ, וְעִם זֶה אֵינוֹ אֶלָּא הוֹד וְזִיו בִּלְבָד.

וּמַה שֶּׁמִּתְלַבֵּשׁ בָּעוֹלָמוֹת בִּפְנִימִיּוּתָם לְהַחֲיוֹתָם הוּא רַק אוֹתִיּוֹת הַדִּבּוּר דִּבְחִינַת מַלְכוּת, וּכְמוֹ שֶׁכָּתוּב בִּדְבַר ה'ᵐᵈ שָׁמַיִם נַעֲשׂוּ, וּכְמוֹ שֶׁכָּתוּב וְאַתָּה מְחַיֶּה‎ᵐᵉ אֶת כּוּלָם, שֶׁהֵם הָאוֹתִיּוֹת מֵאָלֶף עַד ת', וּמְגַלִּים רַק אֶת הָאָרָה חִיצוֹנִית וְגַם זֶה בְּצִמְצוּם אַחַר צִמְצוּם, וּכְמוֹ שֶׁכָּתוּב כְּבוֹד מַלְכוּתְךָᵐᵂ יֹאמֵרוּ וּגְבוּרָתְךָ יְדַבֵּרוּ, בְּחִינַת גְּבוּרוֹת וְצִמְצוּמִים, וְלָכֵן נִתְהַוּוּ עוֹלָמוֹת בִּבְחִינַת יֵשׁ וּמְצִיאוּת.

---

through tav—*give life to them all.* See *Shaar Hayichud Veha'emunah*, ch. 2.

155. **Psalms 145:11.**

156. The verse associates *malchut* with the idea of strength, or *gevurah*, which is synonymous with *tzimtzum* (see above, footnote 52). This is because the "letters of *malchut*" represent the manner in which G-dliness is *contracted*, so as to create worlds that appear to be self-sufficient and self-sustaining.

157. The discourse has thus concluded the theme it began in middle of ch. 3—namely, that it is specifically the attribute of *malchut*, the lowest of the *sefirot*, that allows for

and actualizes the creation of finite beings.

To summarize, there are three levels of *malchut* discussed in this chapter: As it is in *Atzilut* in essence, *hitnasut atzmi*; as it encompasses the lower worlds of *Beriah, Yetzirah* and *Asiyah*, becoming *atik* of *Beriah*; and as it descends into *Beriah, Yetzirah* and *Asiyah* internally, in the form of *letters of speech.*

At this point the discourse concludes its discussion of Creation (i.e., Tishrei), which took place through the attribute of *malchut* and Divine concealment. The next chapter begins expounding the quality of the Exodus from Egypt (i.e., Nissan), which came about through a revelation of G-d's Essence.

7.

However, the verse, *I (*anochi*) am the L-rd your G-d* means that at the giving of the Torah there was an influx from the Essence of *Ein Sof.* For *anochi* denotes sublimity.

This is the difference between *ani* and *anochi* [both of which translate as *I*]. *Ani* denotes humility and *tzimtzum.* As [King David] says, *And I (*ani*) am prayer*—referring to the level of *malchut.*[158] For the level of *malchut* that is supernal speech is a revelation in a manner of *tzimtzum.*[159]

Anochi, by contrast, is the level of *keter,*[160] i.e., the level of sublimity, the Essence of *Ein Sof.*[161] It is not just [Divine] radiance—such as was the case in the creation of the world—but rather a revelation of the Essence of *Ein Sof.*

EXODUS FROM BOUNDARIES

About this the verse says, *[I am the L-rd...] who brought you out of the land of Mitzraim (Egypt).* [This refers to] the exodus from *meitzarim* (limitations) and boundaries, i.e., the *mitzraim* (limitation) of holiness that is the limitation and boundary of the worlds.[162]

---

158. **Psalms 109:4, following the interpretation of** *Zohar* **III:49b.**

In its simple meaning, *I am [a man of] prayer* is David's way of saying that he constantly prays to G-d (*Rashi*).

The *Zohar* interprets the verse as follows: *Prayer* refers to *Knesset Yisrael*, the spiritual "community of Israel"—from where the individual souls descend and are sustained. Thus, David is proclaiming *I am prayer:* I represent *Knesset Yisrael* (before G-d).

Now, *Knesset Yisrael* is also synonymous with *malchut* of *Atzilut.* Based on the *Zohar's* interpretation, then, *Ani (I)* represents—denotes—*malchut* (*Knesset Yisrael*).

Pri Eitz Chaim (beg.) adds that "*Ani* is *malchut*": Just as *malchut* denotes humility, being the lowest of the *sefirot*, likewise *ani* represents humility and *tzimtzum.*

(*I am prayer* is also interpreted as referring to the ascent of *malchut* (*ani*) during prayer. See *Sefer Hamaamarim 5708*, p. 80; p. 244.)

159. As mentioned in the previous chapter, there are various levels of *malchut* of *Atzilut*, the lowest of which is associated with the Divine speech that pervades and vivifies all of existence in an immanent manner. This "speech" of *malchut* is greatly condensed and contracted—a mere glimmer of Divine light, so to

ז.

אָמְנָם, מַה שֶּׁכָּתוּב אָנֹכִי הוי׳ אֱלֹקֶיךָ הוּא, דִּבְמַתַּן תּוֹרָה הֲרֵי זֶה הַמְשָׁכָה מִבְּחִינַת עַצְמִיּוּת אֵין סוֹף, דְּאָנֹכִי מוֹרֶה עַל הָרוֹמְמוּת.

דְּזֶהוּ הַהֶפְרֵשׁ בֵּין אֲנִי לְאָנֹכִי, דַּאֲנִי מוֹרֶה עַל הַשְּׁפְלוּת וְהַצִּמְצוּם, וּכְתִיב וַאֲנִי תְפִלָּה, וְקָאֵי עַל בְּחִינַת מַלְכוּת[160], דִּבְחִינַת הַמַּלְכוּת, בִּבְחִינַת דִּבּוּר הָעֶלְיוֹן, הוּא הַמְשָׁכָה בִּבְחִינַת צִמְצוּם.

אֲבָל אָנֹכִי הוּא בְּחִינַת כֶּתֶר[161], וְהַיְינוּ בְּחִינַת הָרוֹמְמוּת עַצְמוּת דְּאֵין סוֹף, שֶׁאֵין זֶה רַק הָאָרָה בִּלְבַד כְּמוֹ בִּבְרִיאַת הָעוֹלָם, כִּי אִם בְּחִינַת הַמְשָׁכַת הָעַצְמוּת דְּאֵין סוֹף.

וְעַל זֶה אוֹמֵר אֲשֶׁר הוֹצֵאתִיךָ מֵאֶרֶץ מִצְרַיִם, הַיְצִיאָה מֵהַמֵּיצָרִים וּגְבוּלִים, וְהַיְינוּ מִצְרַיִם דִּקְדוּשָׁה[162], שֶׁהוּא הַמֵּיצָר וּגְבוּל דְּעוֹלָמוֹת.

---

speak—so as to animate myriad self-aware beings.

160. See *Likkutei Torah, Leva'er... Venikdashti*, chapter 5 [*Vayikra*, 34d].

See ch. 4 there: "The difference between *anochi* (אנכי) and *ani* (אני) is that *ani* is *malchut*, while *anochi* is synonymous with *ani*, but in a state of glory and exaltedness. It is therefore *keter*, crown [see following footnote]. This is indicated by the additional letter *chaf* (כ) of *anochi*, which is the beginning of the word *keter* (crown) and the word *kavod* (glory)."

161. *Keter* (lit., "crown") is the dimension that lies beyond *Atzilut* and the *sefirot*, and the one most closely associated with the *Ein Sof* (as it is the most primordial emanation from the *Ein Sof*). See *Mystical Concepts in Chassidism*, chapter 3 (*Sefirot*), section 3.

162. As explained above (chapters 3 and 6), it is the condition of limitation (*mitzraim*) in the holy realm—*tzimtzum*, (embodied by) *malchut*—that causes the limitations (*meitzarim*) of the worlds. In a deeper sense, then, the exodus from the limitations of the worlds means an exodus from the limitations of the holy realm; when the condition of *tzimtzum* is nullified, all successive boundaries and limitations are broken down as well.

Through revelation of the Essence of *Ein Sof*, the exodus from the limitation and boundary [of the words] occurs.[163]

For it is from the *mitzraim* of holiness that the *mitzraim* of the "other side"[164] derives, i.e., the limitation and boundary of the lower realm. This refers to the Divine soul that is constrained within the limitation of the animal soul.

When *G-d created the human being upright*,[165] [man was created with] the limitation that the powers of the Divine soul must take on physical manifestation.[166] For the intellect and emotions of the Divine soul are Divine powers; and as they exist above, before their descent to be vested in a body and animal soul, what they perceive is Divinity, literally. But once vested in an animal soul, they behave according to the capacities of the animal soul.

Nonetheless, when the powers of the Divine soul are revealed, the person perceives Divine concepts and is awakened with love and fear [of G-d].[167]

However, it is possible that this being vested [within the animal soul] can completely conceal and cover [the powers of the Divine soul].

This occurs with the strengthening of [the animal soul's] materiality, which diminishes and weakens the powers of the Divine soul.[168] The person then does not grasp Divine concepts; or even if he does grasp them, he does not grasp the Divinity that is within them—he does not perceive the *Divinity* within the concepts. *Intellect is perceived by the mind; Divinity, only by the heart.*

163. G-d's Essence is beyond any spiritual limitations; when Essence is manifest, all limitations cease to be.

164. "Other side" refers to the realm of impurity, which lies opposite the realm of holiness.

165. Ecclesiastes 7:29.

166. As the discourse will soon ex-

plain, this is not necessarily a negative thing; for the purpose—G-d's purpose—in creating man in such a manner is so that the Divine soul *transform* its earthly vessel, the body and animal soul, into something that is receptive to Divinity. When man acts as G-d intended, his Divine soul affects his physical being: he feels love for G-d in his heart, he understands G-dly concepts in his mind, etc. The

וְעַל יְדֵי הַגִּילוּי דְּעַצְמוּת אֵין סוֹף הוּא הַיְצִיאָה מֵהַמֵּיצָר
וּגְבוּל.

דְּהִנֵּה מִמִּצְרַיִם דִּקְדוּשָׁה הוּא שֶׁנַּעֲשָׂה מְצָרִים דִּלְעוּמַת
זֶה, הַיְינוּ הַמֵּיצָר וְהַגְּבוּל שֶׁלְּמַטָּה, וְהוּא דְּהַנֶּפֶשׁ הָאֱלֹקִית הוּא
בְּהַמֵּיצָר דְּנֶפֶשׁ הַבַּהֲמִית.

דְּהִנֵּה כַּאֲשֶׁר הָאֱלֹקִים עָשָׂה אֶת הָאָדָם יָשָׁר, הִנֵּה הַגְבָּלָה
זוֹ מַה שֶׁהַכֹּחוֹת דְּנֶפֶשׁ הָאֱלֹקִית בָּאִים בְּהַגְשָׁמָה, דְּשֵׂכֶל וּמִדּוֹת
דְּנֶפֶשׁ הָאֱלֹקִית הֵן כֹּחוֹת אֱלֹקִים, דְּכָמוֹ שֶׁהֵם לְמַעְלָה טֶרֶם
יְרִידָתָן לְהִתְלַבֵּשׁ בְּגוּף וְנֶפֶשׁ הַבַּהֲמִית הִנֵּה הַהַשָּׂגָה הִיא
שֶׁמַּשִּׂיג אֱלֹקוּת מַמָּשׁ, וּבְהִתְלַבְּשׁוּת בְּנֶפֶשׁ הַבַּהֲמִית בָּאִים כְּפִי
חוּשֵׁי הַנֶּפֶשׁ הַבַּהֲמִית.

וּמִכָּל מָקוֹם הוּא שֶׁהַכֹּחוֹת דְּנֶפֶשׁ הָאֱלֹקִית הֵן בְּהִתְגַּלּוּת,
שֶׁמַּשִּׂיג הַשָּׂגָה אֱלֹקִית וּמִתְעוֹרֵר בְּאַהֲבָה וְיִרְאָה.

אֲבָל בְּהִתְלַבְּשׁוּת זֹאת יָכוֹל לִהְיוֹת שֶׁמַּעֲלִים וּמַסְתִּיר
לְגַמְרֵי.

וְהַיְינוּ בְּהִתְגַּבְּרוּת הַחוּמְרִיּוּת, בָּזֶה מְמַעֵט וּמַחֲלִישׁ הַכֹּחוֹת
דְּנֶפֶשׁ הָאֱלֹקִית, דְּאֵינוּ מַשִּׂיג הַשָּׂגָה אֱלֹקִית, אוֹ גַם כְּשֶׁמַּשִּׂיג
אֵינוּ נִרְגָּשׁ בּוֹ הָאֱלֹקוּת, עֶר דֶּערְהֶערְט נִיט דִי גֶעטְלִיכְקַייט
אִין דֶער הַשָּׂגָה, הַשָּׂגָה וֶוערְט דֶּערְהֶערְט אִין פַארְשְׁטַאנְד,
אוּן גֶעטְלִיכְקַייט וֶוערְט דֶּערְהֶערְט נָאר אִין גֶעפִיל.

---

danger, however, is that the body and animal soul may, over time, become so powerful that they imprison the Divine soul, not allowing it to function as it was intended to. This is the "*mitzraim* of the 'other side.'"

167. Physical man's mind and heart are then imbued with G-dliness—the ultimate fusion of body and soul.

168. *Tukfa degufah chulsha denishmata*—"Strength of body is weakness of soul" (cf. *Zohar* I:180b; 140b). This does not refer to the strengthening of the physical body, but rather to the strengthening of the natural soul vested in the body. Conversely, "strength of (G-dly) soul is weakness of body" (*Sefer Hamaamarim 5709*, p. 63).

But with the strengthening of the materiality of the animal soul, Divinity is no longer perceived. Of this it is said,
My strength has stumbled because of my iniquity[169]: because of
the corruption[170] and crookedness of materiality, the powers
of the Divine soul stumble and grow weak.

All of this occurs because there are limitations and boundaries of holiness; for after much devolution there emerges
limitations of the "other side."[171]

REVELATION OF ESSENCE

In order for the Exodus from Egypt (limitations) to occur, the
revelation of the Essence of the Infinite Light is required.
This idea is seen in the verse, *I will pass through the land of
Egypt*[172]—referring to the revelation of the Essence of the Infinite Light. A similar phrase reads "…before the King of the
kings of kings, the Holy One, blessed be He, revealed Himself to them and redeemed them."[173]

"King of the kings of kings" refers to *malchut* of *Ein Sof*[174]
as it exists subsumed within His Essence. As in the phrase,
"Before the world was created, He and His name were
one"[175]—referring to the level of "His great name."[176]

---

169. **Psalms 31:11.**

170. In the aforementioned verse, the
Hebrew word for *iniquity* is עוני,
which is related to the word עוות, corruption.

171. Every physical phenomenon has
a spiritual source. The same is true of
the material limitations that constrain
the Divine soul: these stem from the
limitation of holiness, i.e., the contraction (*tzimtzum*) of Divinity that
allows for the existence of the worlds.

172. **Exodus 12:12.** Scripture speaks
of the Exodus in the first person (*I
will pass through the land… I will
smite every firstborn… I will carry out

judgments against all the gods of Egypt*),
indicating that G-d Himself—*I*—effected the liberation from *mitzraim*,
limitations. See *Haggadah for Pesach*,
Vayotzi'enu.

173. *Haggadah for Pesach* [*Matzah
Zo*]. This also indicates that the Ex-
odus came about through "the King"
Himself, G-d's Essence.

174. MALCHUT OF EIN SOF. Chasidus
speaks of the concept of *sefirot* existing (in a somewhat "potential"
state) within the wholly G-dly realm
that precedes the first *tzimtzum*, i.e.,
in the realm that precedes the world
of *Atzilut*. The last of these "primordial" *sefirot* is *malchut* of *Ein Sof*,

אֲבָל בְּהִתְגַּבְּרוּת הַחוּמְרִיּוּת דְּנֶפֶשׁ הַבַּהֲמִית אָז אֵינוֹ נִרְגָּשׁ הָאֱלֹקוּת, דְּעַל זֶה נֶאֱמַר כָּשַׁל בַּעֲוֹנֵימ״ט כֹּחִי, דְּעַל יְדֵי הָעֲווֹת וְעִקּוּם שֶׁל הַחוּמְרִיּוּת, נִכְשָׁל וְנֶחֱלָשׁ הַכֹּחוֹת דְּנֶפֶשׁ הָאֱלֹקִית.

שֶׁכָּל זֶה הוּא לְפִי שֶׁיֵּשׁ מְצָרִים וְהַגְבָּלוֹת דִּקְדוּשָּׁה, הִנֵּה עַל יְדֵי רִבּוּי הַהִשְׁתַּלְשְׁלוּת נַעֲשֶׂה מְצָרִים דִּלְעוּמַּת זֶה.

וְלִהְיוֹת יְצִיאַת מִצְרַיִם זֶהוּ עַל יְדֵי הַגִּילוּי דְּעַצְמוּת אוֹר אֵין סוֹף שֶׁנַּעֲשָׂה הַיְצִיאָה מֵהַמֵּצָרִים וּגְבוּלִים, וּכְמוֹ שֶׁכָּתוּב וְעָבַרְתִּי בְאֶרֶץ׳ מִצְרַיִם שֶׁהָיָה גִּילוּי עַצְמוּת אוֹר אֵין סוֹף, וּכְמַאֲמַר עַד שֶׁנִּגְלָהא עֲלֵיהֶם מֶלֶךְ מַלְכֵי הַמְּלָכִים הַקָּדוֹשׁ בָּרוּךְ הוּא וּגְאָלָם.

דְּמֶלֶךְ מַלְכֵי הַמְּלָכִים הוּא בְּחִינַת מַלְכוּת דְּאֵין סוֹף כְּמוֹ שֶׁהוּא כָּלוּל בְּעַצְמוּתוֹ, כְּמַאֲמַר עַד שֶׁלֹּא נִבְרָא הָעוֹלָמנ״ב הָיָה הוּא וּשְׁמוֹ בִּלְבָד, בְּחִינַת שְׁמוֹ הַגָּדוֹל.

---

which ultimately descends to become *atik* of *Atzilut* (much like *malchut* of *Atzilut* becomes *atik* of *Beriah*, as mentioned in the previous chapter). In its pre-descent state, however, this level of *malchut* is completely subsumed within the *Ein Sof*, G-d's Essence. It is this essential dimension of *malchut* that is referred to by the phrase, "King of the kings of kings": i.e., the Exodus occurred through a revelation of G-d's Essence, or more specifically, *malchut* as it is subsumed within Essence. See *Likkutei Torah, Tzav*, 13d; *Torah Or, Miketz*, 35b. See also below, footnote 176.

175. *Pirkei d'Rabbi Eliezer*, chapter 3. There are other versions there as well; however, regarding the pre-ciseness of this version, see the beginning of the introduction to *Shelah*.

Other versions have "before You created the world" or "before the world was," instead of "before the world *was created*." As *Shelah* writes (*Toldot Adam, Beit Havayah*, 3): "There are those who take issue with a similar phrase in the liturgy, 'You are the same before the world was created and You are the same after the world was created...' as it appears in the Ashkenazic version, and they changed it to, 'You, our G-d, are the same before *You created* the world...,' since the passive 'was created' can mean, G-d forbid, that the world

TO YOU

> This revelation [of the Essence of the *Ein Sof*] is directed spe-
> cifically to the souls of Israel.[177]
>
> This, then, is the meaning of the words, *This month [is for
> you…]*: *month* denotes revelation.[178] So *this month*, or *this rev-
> elation*, is *for you* specifically—only for the souls of Israel.
>
> This is because the souls of Israel stem from the inner di-
> mension of the Infinite Light, unlike all other creatures whose
> creation stems only from the supernal speech of the "ten ut-
> terances."[179] Souls, however, arose in [supernal] thought.[180]
> Thought in this context refers to the essential thought of the
> inner dimension and Essence of the *Ein Sof,* blessed be He,
> which transcends the general thought that is upon the worlds
> and the creatures on the highest level.[181]
>
> It was therefore the souls of Israel who were "consulted"

---

came into being from some other source other than G-d…. However, in all the books of the Kabbalists, the version is 'was created.' I therefore say that theirs is the true version…. This version can also be found in *Tosfot* (*Berachot* 46a, s.v. *Kol*; *Pesachim* 104b, s.v. *Kol*) and in *Tur* (*Orach Chaim* 46)." *Shelah* goes on to provide a lengthy Kabbalistic explanation of the version he deems correct.

176. Before the world was conceived, *malchut* was subsumed within the Essence of *Ein Sof*. Of that reality it is said that G-d and His name—*malchut*—are one. After the earliest, spiritual stages of Creation—i.e., the concealment of Divine light that allowed for the process of creation to begin (*Sefer Hamaamarim Melukat,* vol. 3, p. 275)—*malchut* descends into the lower worlds, into "exile," and G-d and His name (*malchut*) are

no longer one.

When *malchut* is subsumed within the *Ein Sof* it is like the rays of the sun prior to their emergence from the sun. They certainly exist within the sun, but they exist in a state of "non-existence," completely nullified to the sun itself. Similarly, *malchut* of *Ein Sof* exists in a state of non-existence (*Sefer Hamaamarim Melukat,* vol. 6, p. 94). Through *tzimtzum,* which is caused through the name *Elokim, malchut* becomes relatively "existent" and is no longer completely one with the *Ein Sof.* However, since the concealment caused by the *tzimtzum* is real only to us, the truth is that even now G-d and His name are one just as they were prior to the *tzimtzum* (*Sefer Hamaamarim Melukat,* vol. 3, p. 61).

177. It is specifically to (and for) the souls of Israel that the Essence of the *Ein Sof* is revealed, since, as will be ex-

וְהַגִּילוּי הַזֶּה הוּא לְנִשְׁמוֹת יִשְׂרָאֵל דַּוְקָא.

וְזֶהוּ הַחִדּוּשׁ הַזֶּה, דְּהַחִדּוּשׁ הוּא גִּילוּי, הִנֵּה הַחִדּוּשׁ הַזֶּה הַגִּילוּי הַזֶּה הוּא לָכֶם דַּוְקָא, רַק לְנִשְׁמוֹת יִשְׂרָאֵל.

דְּנִשְׁמוֹת יִשְׂרָאֵל הֵן מִפְּנִימִיּוּת אוֹר אֵין סוֹף, וְלֹא כְּמוֹ הַנִּבְרָאִים שֶׁהִתְהַוּוּתָם הוּא רַק מִבְּחִינַת דִּבּוּר הָעֶלְיוֹן שֶׁבַּעֲשָׂרָה מַאֲמָרוֹת, אֲבָל נִשְׁמוֹת עָלוּ[י] בְּמַחֲשָׁבָה, וְהָעֲלִיָּה הִיא בְּהַמַּחֲשָׁבָה עַצְמִית דִּפְנִימִיּוּת וְעַצְמוּת אֵין סוֹף בָּרוּךְ הוּא שֶׁלְּמַעְלָה מֵהַמַּחֲשָׁבָה כְּלָלִית שֶׁעַל הָעוֹלָמוֹת וְהַנִּבְרָאִים בְּמַדְרֵיגָה הַיּוֹתֵר עֶלְיוֹנָה.

שֶׁלָּכֵן הִנֵּה הַהַמְלָכָה עַל הָרָצוֹן בִּבְרִיאַת הָעוֹלָם הָיָה

---

plained, these souls stem from G-d's Essence.

178. The Jewish calendar follows the lunar cycle. Thus, the Hebrew word for month is *chodesh*, which means "new," referring to the new moon that appears at the beginning of each month (see *Ibn Ezra* on Exodus 12:2, et al.). *Chodesh, month*, therefore denotes revelation—revelation of a new "light."

179. See above, chapter 2, and footnote 41.

Creation through supernal speech occurs from the level of *malchut* of *Atzilut*. The souls of Israel, however, stem not from supernal speech but from G-d's essential thought, which, as the discourse will explain, refers to the Essence of the *Ein Sof*.

180. **See above, discourse entitled *Ki Imcha Mekor Chaim*, chapter 7** [*Sefer*

Hamaamarim 5700, p. 17]. There the footnote reads: "*Bereishit Rabbah*, beginning of chapter 1 [section 4]. See also *Likkutei Torah, Biur* on *Yonati Bechagvei* [*Shir Hashirim*, 17c ff.]."

181. All of creation stems ultimately from G-d's "thought," the thought that precedes the speech that actually creates. For just as a mortal's speech stems from his thought, as "a person can speak only such words that he has already spoken previously and that were in his thought a great many time" (*Iggeret Hakodesh*, 19, end), similarly, G-d's speech stems from his supernal "thought." But this is an all-encompassing thought that relates to Creation—that which is created by speech. The thought from which the souls of Israel stem is a much deeper thought, an *essential* thought, one that is completely beyond Creation.

regarding the desire to create the worlds, as the saying, "With whom did He consult? With the souls of the righteous."[182]

It is for this reason that the souls of Israel are vessels for the Essence of the blessed *Ein Sof*, and elicit the Essence through their [spiritual] service of Torah and *mitzvot*.[183]

And this revelation [of Essence] produces the exodus from limitations and boundaries.[184]

It therefore says, *[I am the L-rd...] who brought you out of the land of Egypt (Mitzraim)*, and not *[I am the L-rd...] who created heaven and earth*.[185] For the creation of heaven and earth stems only from [Divine] radiance, through which the worlds became limited and actual, and with much devolution bore the *mitzraim* of the "other side."

The revelation of *anochi*, by contrast, gave way to the *Exodus* from *mitzraim*.[186]

NISSAN AND TISHREI

This is the general difference between Nissan and Tishrei. Tishrei is the first of the months of the year.[187] The twelve months of the year[188] correspond to the four camps of the *Shechinah* (Divine Presence), the twelve oxen of the lower chariot of the level of *malchut*.[189]

---

182. See *Rut Rabbah*, 2:3. See further from *Sefer Hamaamarim 5703*, p. 9: "G-d foresaw the pleasure that He would receive from the souls performing their Divine service below." This underscores the lofty source of the souls of Israel, who stem from the essential thought of the *Ein Sof* that precedes Creation; for it was with these very souls that G-d decided, so to speak, whether or not to create the worlds.

183. Since the souls of Israel stem from the essential thought contained within the Essence of the *Ein Sof*, they are therefore able to receive (and contain) a revelation of G-d's Es-

sence. Moreover, they can *elicit* Essence with their Divine service. See *Sefer Hamaamarim 5700*, p. 18.

184. See above, footnote 163.

185. The discourse now addresses the question raised above, in chapter 2: Why does G-d "introduce" Himself at the giving of the Torah as the G-d *who brought you out of the land of Egypt*, and not as the G-d *who created heaven and earth* (which seems to be a much greater feat)?

186. Therefore, at the giving of the Torah, when G-d reveals His Essence—*anochi*—He identifies Him-

עִם הַנְּשָׁמוֹת, כְּמַאֲמָר בְּמִי נִמְלַךְ בְּנִשְׁמוֹתֵיהֶן שֶׁל צַדִּיקִים.

וּמֵהַאי טַעֲמָא הִנֵּה נִשְׁמוֹת יִשְׂרָאֵל הֵם כֵּלִים לְעַצְמוּת אֵין סוֹף בָּרוּךְ הוּא, וּמַמְשִׁיכוֹת אֶת הָעַצְמוּת עַל יְדֵי עֲבוֹדָתָם בְּתוֹרָה וּמִצְוֹת.

וּמִגִּילּוּי זֶה הוּא הַיְצִיאָה מֵהַמֵּיצָרִים וּגְבוּלִים.

וְלָכֵן נֶאֱמַר אֲשֶׁר הוֹצֵאתִיךָ מֵאֶרֶץ מִצְרַיִם וְלֹא נֶאֱמַר אֲשֶׁר בָּרָאתִי שָׁמַיִם וָאָרֶץ, דִּבְרִיאַת שָׁמַיִם וָאָרֶץ הוּא מֵהָאָרָה לְבַד, שֶׁעַל יְדֵי זֶה נַעֲשׂוּ הָעוֹלָמוֹת בִּבְחִינַת הַגְבָּלָה וּמְצִיאוּת יֵשׁ, וּבְרִיבּוּי הִשְׁתַּלְשְׁלוּת הִנֵּה מִזֶּה נַעֲשֶׂה מִצְרַיִם דִּלְעוּמַת זֶה.

אָמְנָם מֵהַגִּילּוּי דְּאָנֹכִי נַעֲשֶׂה יְצִיאַת מִצְרָיִם.

שֶׁזֶּהוּ כְּלָלוּת הַהֶפְרֵשׁ בֵּין נִיסָן וְתִשְׁרֵי. דְּתִשְׁרֵי רֹאשׁ חָדְשֵׁי הַשָּׁנָה, דְּי״ב חָדְשֵׁי הַשָּׁנָה הֵם ד' מַחֲנוֹת שְׁכִינָה, י״ב בָּקָר דְּמֶרְכַּבְתָּא תַּתָּאָה דִּבְחִינַת מַלְכוּת.

---

self as the G-d *who brought you out of the land of Egypt (Mitzraim)*, since revelation of Essence spawns Exodus, not Creation.

187. As mentioned at the beginning of the discourse, Tishrei is the first month of the year as far as *Creation* is concerned, being that Creation was culminated on the first day of Tishrei (with the creation of Adam). Tishrei, the first month of Creation, thus represents *malchut*, the animating force of Creation.

188. See *Zohar* III:277b, end; *Pardes, Shaar* 21, chapters 6-7.

189. In Scripture's account of King Solomon's construction of the *Beit Hamikdash*, we read (II Chronicles 4:2-4): *He made the "sea"* (a copper tank that was filled with water, used by the Kohanim for ritual immersion—ibid., verse 6) *of cast metal... It stood upon twelve oxen: three facing north, three facing west, three facing south, three facing east. The "sea" was on top of them....* Kabbalah and Chasidus explain that these elements—the *twelve oxen* and the *"sea"...on top of them*—have their parallel in the supernal realms.

"*Sea*" refers to the *sefirah* of *malchut*; for *malchut's* function is *tzimtzum* and concealment, much like the

So "when G-d chose His world, He established [in it] *firsts of months*,"[190] so that the revelation[191] should flow into the root and source of the worlds.[192] But in general, this is only [a revelation of Divine] radiance. "When G-d chose Jacob and his sons," however, "He established for them a month of redemption," the month of Nissan, which is a revelation of G-d's blessed Essence.[193]

---

sea that conceals whatever is found within it (*Likkutei Torah, Vayikra,* 16c). The *twelve oxen,* divided into four groups of three, refer to the four camps of the *Shechinah* (Divine Presence)—the four groups, or "camps," of angels in the world of *Beriah. Three facing north* signifies the camp of the angel Gabriel (*gevurah*); *three facing south* signifies the camp of the angel Michael (*chesed*); etc. And these *twelve oxen,* the four camps of the *shechinah,* stem from *malchut,* the *"sea"…on top of them*—for it is *malchut* that creates limitation and distinction, plurality (see *Likkutei Torah, Bamidbar,* 68c).

Furthermore, the *Zohar* and *Pardes* (ibid.) draw a correlation between the *twelve oxen* and the twelve months of the year (see *Likkutei Torah, Derushim l'Rosh Hashanah,* 53d). This indicates that the distinction of twelve separate months likewise stems from *malchut.* Thus, Tishrei, the first of the twelve months of the year, embodies the limiting of Divine light, the revelation of but a small ray of Divinity, *malchut.*

וּמְשֻׁבָּחַר בְּעוֹלָמוֹ קָבַע רָאשֵׁי חֳדָשִׁים שֶׁיּוּמְשַׁךְ הַגִּילּוּי
בְּשֹׁרֶשׁ וּמְקוֹר הָעוֹלָמוֹת, אֲבָל בִּכְלָלוּתוֹ הוּא בְּחִינַת הָאָרָה
לְבָד. אָמְנָם מְשֻׁבָּחַר בְּיַעֲקֹב וּבָנָיו קָבַע לָהֶם חֹדֶשׁ שֶׁל גְּאוּלָה,
חֹדֶשׁ נִיסָן, שֶׁהוּא גִּילּוּי הָעַצְמוּת בָּרוּךְ הוּא.

---

190. *Shemot Rabbah* 15:11, cited above, chapter 1.

191. I.e., the Divine revelation that spawns Creation (*malchut*).

192. This perhaps explains why the redemption began in Tishrei with the cessation of harsh labor (see above, footnote 22)—for even Tishrei experiences some degree of Divine revelation, just not of the level that would effect the complete redemption.

193. For, as explained at length above, redemption—Exodus—occurs only with the revelation of G-d's Essence.

The following table sums up the two levels that are discussed in the discourse:

Tishrei	Nissan
Creation	Exodus/Sinai/Israel
Elokim/Ani	*Anochi*
malchut	*Keter*/Essence of *Ein Sof*

8.

And this is the meaning of, *This month is for you the first of months; it is, for you, the first of the months of the year.*[194]

There are *months of the year, month* denoting revelation.[195] However, this [is a revelation that] takes place only in the *months of the year.*[196] Then there are *months* without designation, which are revelations that are loftier than *months of the year.*[197] And this is the meaning of *this month*—i.e., *this* revelation is only for you *and not for the foreigner with you.*[198]

The nature of this revelation is *first of months.* Not only is it of the category of revelations of *months*—i.e., *months* without designation, which denotes a general revelation, unlike *months of the year,* which denotes particular revelations—furthermore, the novelty and revelation of *this month* is that it is *the first of months:* Within the general and essential category of *months,* it is the *first.*[199]

And this revelation will be *for you*—specifically—*the first,* even during *the months of the year.*[200]

Within *the months of the year,* the [general] first is Tishrei, which is the first month for years.[201] Hence, Yonatan com-

---

194. At the beginning of the discourse it was noted that there are two distinct dynamics mentioned in this verse: 1) *[First of] months*; and 2) *months of the year.* Based on the distinction that has been drawn between Creation (Tishrei) and Exodus (Nissan), i.e., between the level of Divine radiance that relates to the worlds and the Essence of *Ein Sof* that completely transcends the worlds, the discourse now returns to its interpretation of this verse, and explains thus:

The term *months,* in general, refers to Divine revelation. More specifically, there are two types of revelation: 1) Revelation of Divine *radiance*; and 2) revelation of *Essence.* And these are the two dimensions mentioned in this verse: *Months of the year* refers to the revelation of Divine *radiance* (revelation that pertains to Creation), while *months* (without any qualifications) refers to the revelation of the Essence of *Ein Sof.*

195. See above, footnote 178.

196. I.e., it is a revelation of the particular Divine energy that is associated with the natural, yearly cycle of Creation—the revelation of Divine radiance, *malchut.*

197. I.e., the revelation of the Essence of *Ein Sof,* which completely transcends Creation. This lofty revelation (*months*) is not qualified by any restrictive term (like *of the year*).

‫ח.‬

‫וְזֶהוּ הַחֹדֶשׁ הַזֶּה לָכֶם רֹאשׁ חֳדָשִׁים, רִאשׁוֹן הוּא לָכֶם לְחָדְשֵׁי הַשָּׁנָה.‬

‫דְּהִנֵּה יֵשׁ חָדְשֵׁי הַשָּׁנָה, דְּחֹדֶשׁ הוּא עִנְיַן הַגִּילּוּי, אֲבָל גִּילּוּי זֶה הוּא רַק בְּחָדְשֵׁי הַשָּׁנָה. וְיֵשׁ חֳדָשִׁים סְתָם, גִּילּוּיִם גְּבוֹהִים יוֹתֵר מֵחָדְשֵׁי הַשָּׁנָה. וְזֶהוּ הַחֹדֶשׁ הַזֶּה, דְּגִילּוּי זֶה הוּא רַק לָכֶם וְלֹא לְזָר אִתְּכֶם.‬

‫וּמַהוּתוֹ שֶׁל הַגִּילּוּי הוּא רֹאשׁ חֳדָשִׁים, דְּלֹא זוֹ בִּלְבָד שֶׁהוּא מִסּוּג הַגִּילּוּי דְּחֳדָשִׁים, לְשׁוֹן חִידּוּשׁ סְתָם, חִידּוּשׁ כְּלָלִי, דְּאֵינוּ כְּמוֹ חָדְשֵׁי הַשָּׁנָה שֶׁהֵם חִדּוּשִׁים פְּרָטִים, אֶלָּא שֶׁהוּא חִידּוּשׁ כְּלָלִי, אֶלָּא עוֹד זֹאת דְּחִידּוּשׁ וְגִילּוּי זֶה דְּהַחֹדֶשׁ הַזֶּה הוּא רֹאשׁ חֳדָשִׁים, דְּבַסּוּג הַגִּילּוּיִם כְּלָלִיִּים וְעַצְמִיִּים דְּחֳדָשִׁים הוּא הָרֹאשׁ.‬

‫וְגִילּוּי זֶה יִהְיֶה לָכֶם רִאשׁוֹן דַּוְקָא גַּם בְּחָדְשֵׁי הַשָּׁנָה.‬

‫דְּבְחָדְשֵׁי הַשָּׁנָה הִנֵּה הָרֹאשׁ הוּא תִּשְׁרֵי שֶׁהוּא רֹאשׁ‬

---

198. Proverbs 5:17. *Shemot Rabbah* 15:23 quotes this to expound on the opening verse of the present discourse: "*This month is for you*—thus it is written, *they will be only for you and not for the foreigner with you.*" This implies that the concept of Rosh Chodesh was given only to Israel.

On a deeper level, in the context of this discourse, this is understood to mean that the revelation of (undesignated) *months*—the Essence of *Ein Sof*—is exclusively for the souls of Israel, since they are rooted in G-d's Essence, as explained in the previous chapter.

199. Not only is this revelation be-

yond Creation—*months* (without any qualifications)—it is the deepest, highest form of revelation that transcends Creation: *first of months*.

200. I.e., for the souls of Israel, the Essence of *Ein Sof* is manifest within the very Creation it transcends. Hence the verse's second clause: *It is, for you, the first of the months of the year.*

201. As mentioned at the beginning of the discourse, the Jewish year begins on Rosh Hashanah, the first day of Tishrei. Tishrei is thus the first month as far as the counting of years is concerned.

ments "that the ancient ones used to call [Tishrei] the first month."[202] For in the months of the creation of the world, which represent the influx of only [Divine] radiance, Tishrei is the first.[203] But now [says Yonatan], after the Exodus from Egypt and the giving of the Torah, when the revelation is of the Essence of *Ein Sof*, Nissan is the *first of months* and Tishrei is the seventh month.

THE SEVENTH

Now, it is known that "all sevenths are precious."[204] It follows, then, that Tishrei has two distinctions: 1) As far as the months of creation, it is the first; 2) as far as the months of redemption—where Nissan is the first—Tishrei is the seventh, and all sevenths are precious.

This explains the reasoning of R. Eliezer, who maintains that our forefathers were redeemed from Egypt in Nissan, and we are destined to be redeemed in Tishrei—because of the distinction of the seventh month.[205]

R. Yehoshua, however, maintains that that in Nissan our forefathers were redeemed from Egypt, and in Nissan we are destined to be redeemed, as it says, *As in the days that you left Egypt I will show you wonders.*[206] Just as the first redemption from Egypt occurred in Nissan, so, too, *I will show you wonders* in the final redemption, with the coming of Moshiach the righteous redeemer, speedily in our days, Amen—the redemption will occur during Nissan. And in *Midrash Rabbah* the Sages follow[207] the opinion of R. Yehoshua, that in Nissan

---

202. *Targum Yonatan* on I Kings 8:2, cited above, chapter 1.

203. Tishrei embodies the natural cycle of Creation, the influx of mere Divine radiance.

204. *Vayikra Rabbah* 29:11.
   Midrash ibid.: "All sevenths are precious... Among the Patriarchs—Abraham, Isaac, Jacob, Levi, Kohath,

Amram and Moses—the seventh is precious, as the verse says (Exodus 19:3), *Moses ascended to G-d.* Among sons the seventh is precious, as it says (I Chronicles 2:15), *David, the seventh* [i.e., David was the seventh and most "precious" son of Yishai]... Among years the seventh is precious [i.e., the Sabbatical year]... Among sabbaticals the seventh is precious [i.e., the Jubilee year]... Among days

לַשָּׁנִים, וְזֶהוּ שֶׁתִּרְגֵּם יוֹנָתָן דְּעַתִּיקַיָּא קָרָן לֵיהּ יַרְחָא קַדְמָאָה, דְּבְחָדְשִׁים דְּבְרִיאַת הָעוֹלָם, שֶׁהֵם הַמְשָׁכַת הָאָרָה בִּלְבָד, תִּשְׁרֵי הוּא רֹאשׁ, וּכְעַן אַחַר יְצִיאַת מִצְרַיִם וּמַתַּן תּוֹרָה, שֶׁהַגִּילוּי הוּא עַצְמוּת אֵין סוֹף, הִנֵּה נִיסָן הוּא רֹאשׁ חָדְשִׁים וְתִשְׁרֵי הוּא יַרְחָא שְׁבִיעָאָה.

וְיָדוּעַ דְּכָל הַשְּׁבִיעִין חֲבִיבִין[4], אִם כֵּן בְּתִשְׁרֵי יֵשׁ בּוֹ ב׳ מַעֲלוֹת: א׳ דְּבְחָדְשִׁים דְּבְרִיאַת הָעוֹלָם הוּא הָרֹאשׁ, וְהַב׳ דְּבְחָדְשִׁים דִּגְאוּלָה דְּנִיסָן שֶׁנִּיסָן הוּא הָרֹאשׁ הֲרֵי תִּשְׁרֵי הוּא הַשְּׁבִיעִי, דְּכָל הַשְּׁבִיעִין חֲבִיבִין.

וְזֶהוּ טַעֲמוֹ שֶׁל רַבִּי אֱלִיעֶזֶר דְּסְבִירָא לֵיהּ דְּבְנִיסָן נִגְאֲלוּ אֲבוֹתֵינוּ מִמִּצְרַיִם וּבְתִשְׁרֵי עֲתִידִין לְהִגָּאֵל, מִפְּנֵי מַעֲלַת הַשְּׁבִיעִי.

וְרַבִּי יְהוֹשֻׁעַ סְבִירָא לֵיהּ דְּבְנִיסָן נִגְאֲלוּ אֲבוֹתֵינוּ מִמִּצְרַיִם וּבְנִיסָן עֲתִידִין לְהִגָּאֵל, שֶׁנֶּאֱמַר כִּימֵי צֵאתְךָ[4] מֵאֶרֶץ מִצְרַיִם אַרְאֶנּוּ נִפְלָאוֹת, דִּכְשֵׁם שֶׁהַגְּאוּלָה הָרִאשׁוֹנָה מִמִּצְרַיִם הָיְתָה בְּנִיסָן הִנֵּה כֵּן אַרְאֶנּוּ נִפְלָאוֹת בַּגְּאוּלָה הָאַחֲרוֹנָה בְּבִיאַת הַמָּשִׁיחַ גּוֹאֵל צֶדֶק בִּמְהֵרָה בְיָמֵינוּ אָמֵן תִּהְיֶה הַגְּאוּלָה בְּנִיסָן. וּבְמִדְרָשׁ הִכְרִיעוּ וְסָתְמוּ כְּרַבִּי

---

the seventh is precious [i.e., Shabbat]… Among months the seventh is precious…."

205. Once the Jewish people were redeemed during Nissan, Nissan became the first month of redemption.

At that point Tishrei gained the status of being the seventh after Nissan. The next redemption, in R. Eliezer's view, will therefore take place in the seventh (and most precious) month after Nissan: Tishrei.

206. **Micah 7:15.** This verse speaks of the future redemption in the Messianic Era, and compares it to the Exodus from Egypt. R. Yehoshua uses this parallel with regards to the *time* of the redemption: Just as the Exodus occurred in Nissan, the future redemption will likewise occur in Nissan.

207. See above, chapter 1 and footnote 13.

our forefathers were redeemed from Egypt, and in Nissan we are destined to be redeemed.

Now, it would seem that Tishrei has the additional distinction of being the seventh.[208] Nevertheless, it is their view that the redemption will occur in Nissan [and this requires explanation].

DAYS OF AWE

There are several reasons for this. Firstly, as far as the *sefirot* are concerned, Nissan is *chesed*, kindness, and Tishrei is *gevurah*, severity[209]; i.e., Tishrei is a time of judgment and justice. We therefore do not recite the phrase "festivals for rejoicing"[210] on Rosh Hashanah, as it is a time of justice.

And although the mitzvah of sounding the *shofar*, representative of repentance,[211] causes [G-d] to rise from the throne of Judgment and sit on the throne of Mercy and to have mercy on His people,[212] nevertheless, the time itself is a time of judgment and justice, when all created beings pass before Him in judgment and justice.

---

208. I.e., in addition to Tishrei being the first month of the year as far as Creation is concerned, it is the seventh from Nissan, and therefore has the quality of being "precious."

209. See *Zohar* (II:186a): "*This month is for you... following the order of the letters—aviv* (spring).... The seventh month is [spelled] from the end of the letters....'" Nissan, which always occurs (in the Holy Land) in the spring, is referred to in Scripture as the month of *aviv*, the month of springtime (see Exodus 13:4, 34:18; Deuteronomy 16:1). Now, the Hebrew letters of *aviv* (אביב) follow the order of the *alef-bet*: the first letter is *alef* (א), which is the first letter of the *alef-bet*; the second letter of *aviv* is *vet* (ב), the second letter of the *alef-bet*. By contrast, the let-

ters that form the seventh month, Tishrei (תשרי), follow the *reverse* order of the *alef-bet*: the first letter is *tav* (ת), the final letter of the *alef-bet*; the second letter is *shin* (ש), the second-to-last letter of the *alef-bet*; the third letter is *resh* (ר), the third-to-last letter of the *alef-bet*.

The *Zohar* also states (ibid. 51b) that "when the letters...appear in order...they are in *chesed*.... [When they appear] in reverse order...they are in *gevurah*." The letters of the word *aviv*, which refers to Nissan, appear in order, indicating that Nissan is a time of *chesed*. The letters of the word Tishrei, however, appear in reverse order, indicating that it is a time of *gevurah*.

See Arizal's *Likkutei Torah, parshat Vayeitzei*, s.v. *Inyan hazayin kochvei lechet*: "From Nissan to

יְהוֹשֻׁעַ, דְּבִנִיסָן נִגְאֲלוּ אֲבוֹתֵינוּ מִמִּצְרַיִם וּבְנִיסָן עֲתִידִין לְהִגָּאֵל.

וְלִכְאוֹרָה הִנֵּה בְּתִשְׁרֵי יֵשׁ יִתְרוֹן מַעֲלָה דְּשְׁבִיעִי, וּמִכָּל מָקוֹם דַּעְתָּם דְּשֶׁבְּנִיסָן תִּהְיֶה הַגְּאוּלָה.

אַךְ הָעִנְיָן הוּא, דְּהִנֵּה יֵשׁ בָּזֶה כַּמָּה טְעָמִים. הָא׳, שֶׁבְּעִנְיַן הַסְּפִירוֹת הִנֵּה נִיסָן הוּא חֶסֶד וְתִשְׁרֵי גְבוּרָה[י], וְהוּא זְמַן הַדִּין וּמִשְׁפָּט, דְּלָכֵן אֵין אוֹמְרִים[יא] מוֹעֲדִים לְשִׂמְחָה בְּרֹאשׁ הַשָּׁנָה לְפִי שֶׁהוּא זְמַן הַמִּשְׁפָּט.

וַהֲגַם שֶׁעַל יְדֵי מִצְוַת תְּקִיעַת שׁוֹפָר, שֶׁעִנְיָנָהּ תְּשׁוּבָה[יב], פּוֹעֲלִים לִהְיוֹת עוֹמֵד מִכִּסֵּא דִין וְיוֹשֵׁב עַל כִּסֵּא רַחֲמִים וּמְרַחֵם עַל עַמּוֹ, הִנֵּה בְּכָל זֶה הֲרֵי עֶצֶם הַזְּמַן הוּא זְמַן הַדִּין וּמִשְׁפָּט, דְּכָל בָּאֵי עוֹלָם עוֹבְרִים לְפָנָיו יִתְבָּרֵךְ בְּדִין וּמִשְׁפָּט.

Elul...*zecharim* [maleness]...*chesed, gevurah, tiferet, netzach, hod, yesod...* And from Tishrei...the *gevurot* of rains, *or chozer, nukva* [rebounding light and femaleness, i.e., *malchut*]." The six months from Nissan to Elul correspond to the six *sefirot* of *chesed* through *yesod*, with Nissan corresponding to *chesed*. Tishrei, however, corresponds to *malchut* and the aspect of *gevurah*.

(This requires further study in light of Arizal's statement that seems to contradict the above: see *Taamei Hamitzvot, parshat Bo*—cited in *Ateret Rosh* [by Rabbi DovBer of Lubavitch], discourse on *Aseret Yemei Teshuvah*, beg.; *Pri Eitz Chaim, Shaar Rosh Hashanah,* chapter 4; *Shaar Hakavanot, Inyan Rosh Hashanaah, derush* 1; end of *Nahar Shalom*—at the end of *Eitz Chaim* in the Warsaw version.)

See also *Kehilat Yaakov* on the topic of the 12 months.

210. *Shulchan Aruch Harav* [*Orach Chaim*] 582:10. This requires some further research.

Shulchan Aruch ibid.: "On Rosh Hashanah and Yom Kippur we do not recite 'festivals for rejoicing, holidays and seasons for gladness' [a phrase that is recited in the Amidah on Pesach, Shavuot and Sukkot], because these days were not given for rejoicing and gladness...."

Rosh Hashanah and Yom Kippur are not festive holidays, but rather days of awe, repentance and judgment. This underscores the fact that Tishrei is associated with the *sefirah* of *gevurah*, severity and judgment.

211. See below, discourse entitled *Shofar Shel Rosh Hashanah* [*Sefer Hamaamarim 5702*, p. 3].

212. See *Vayikra Rabbah* 29:6.

These days are called Days of Awe,[213] for there is then the revelation of the [supernal] dimension of awesomeness. And it is for this reason that these days require an additional amount of meticulousness, to be very careful with the beautifications of the *mitzvot*,[214] since the days themselves occur during a time of the revelation of the dimension of awesomeness. The time is, in and of itself, awesome.

Hence, the redemption will take place in Nissan, a time of *chesed*.[215]

RAIN AND DEW

Secondly, the revelation that occurred on Pesach came as an unprovoked supernal inspiration, as in the statement: "Why do we eat this matzah? Because the dough of our ancestors did not have time to become leaven before the King of the kings of kings, the Holy One, blessed be He, revealed Himself to them and redeemed them."[216]

So the revelation came as an unprovoked supernal inspiration, as in the verse, *My Beloved is mine and I am His.*[217]

[To explain:] There are two types of supernal in-

---

213. DAYS OF AWE. This traditional phrase refers specifically to the days of Rosh Hashanah and Yom Kippur, and more generally to the first ten days of Tishrei (which are also called the Ten Days of Repentance). These days are called Days of Awe as it is a fearful and awesome time, when the entire world stands before G-d in judgment. On a deeper level, we feel this intense awe precisely because the supernal dimension of awesomeness is manifest during this time.

214. *Hidurei mitzvah* in the Hebrew. Beyond the actual performance of the *mitzvot*, there is the concept of *hidur mitzvah*—performing the mitzvah in a more beautiful manner than that which *halachah* mandates.

On the verse (Exodus 15:2), *This is my G-d, and I will glorify Him*, the Talmud comments (*Shabbat* 133b), "Become glorified before Him in *mitzvot*. Make before him a beautiful *sukkah*, a beautiful *lulav*, a beautiful *shofar*, beautiful *tzitzit*, a beautiful Torah scroll...." *Rashi* comments on *Bava Kama* 9b that this verse is the source of *hidur mitzvah*, beautifying the *mitzvot*. Indeed, as the Talmud states there, "one should spend an additional one-third to beautify the mitzvah."

During the Days of Awe we are enjoined to be more meticulous in fulfilling *mitzvot* in the best possible manner, and to be careful in areas which we might have previously been lax. See, for example, *Shulchan Aruch*

וְנִקְרָאִים יָמִים נוֹרָאִים, שֶׁאָז הוּא גִילוּי בְּחִינַת נוֹרָא,
וּמֵהַאי טַעֲמָא הִנֵּה בְּיָמִים אֵלּוּ צְרִיכִים זְהִירוּת יְתֵרָה לְדַקְדֵּק
בְּיוֹתֵר בְּהִידּוּרֵי מִצְוָה, לִהְיוֹת הַיָּמִים עַצְמָם הֵם בִּזְמַן גִילוּי
בְּחִינַת נוֹרָא, הַזְמַן הוּא נוֹרָא בְּעַצְמוֹ.

וְעַל כֵּן תִּהְיֶה הַגְּאוּלָה בְּנִיסָן שֶׁהוּא בְּחִינַת חֶסֶד.

הַב׳, דְּהִנֵּה הַגִילוּי דְפֶּסַח הָיָה בְּאִתְעֲרוּתָא דִלְעֵלָּא
מִצַּד עַצְמָהּ, וּכְמַאֲמַר מַצָּה זוֹ שֶׁאָנוּ אוֹכְלִים עַל שׁוּם מָה,
עַל שׁוּם שֶׁלֹּא הִסְפִּיק בְּצֵקֶת שֶׁל אֲבוֹתֵינוּ לְהַחֲמִיץ עַד
שֶׁנִגְלָה עֲלֵיהֶם מֶלֶךְ מַלְכֵי הַמְּלָכִים הַקָּדוֹשׁ בָּרוּךְ הוּא
וּגְאָלָם.

הֲרֵי שֶׁהַגִילוּי הָיָה עַל יְדֵי אִתְעֲרוּתָא דִלְעֵלָּא מִצַּד עַצְמָהּ,
כְּמוֹ שֶׁכָּתוּב דּוֹדִי לִי²¹⁷ וַאֲנִי לוֹ.

דְּבְאִתְעֲרוּתָא דִלְעֵלָּא הֲרֵי יֵשׁ ב׳ בְּחִינוֹת וּמַדְרֵיגוֹת, הָא׳

Harav (603:1): "Even one who generally eats bread baked by non-Jewish
bakers—which is halachically per-
mitted—should refrain from doing so
during the Ten Days of Repentance"
(i.e., from Rosh Hashanah to Yom
Kippur).

215. Since Tishrei is a time of judgment and awe (*gevurah*), it is not the
most fitting time for redemption, an
act of Divine benevolence and closeness. Our Sages therefore stated that
the future redemption will take place
in Nissan—a time of *chesed*.

216. *Haggadah for Pesach* [*Matzah
Zo*]. This passage indicates that G-d's
revelation at the Exodus came about
completely unprovoked—"the Holy

One…revealed Himself to them and
redeemed them."

217. **Song of Songs 2:16. See below,
discourse entitled *Ani Ledodi* [*Sefer
Hamaamarim 5700*, p. 150].**
My Beloved (i.e., G-d) *is mine* refers
to G-d reaching out to the Jewish people; and in response, *I am His*—the
Jewish people turn to G-d. This is the
dynamic of Nissan. By contrast, the
verse, *I am my Beloved's and He is mine*
(ibid. 6:3) refers to the opposite dynamic, that of Elul/Tishrei, where the
Jewish people reach out to G-d and
He in response turns to them. On Pesach, G-d turned to us without any
provocation on our part. This is called
itaruta deli'ayla mitzad atzmo: an unprovoked supernal inspiration.

spirations. The first type is one that is provoked by an inspiration from the lower worlds. An example of this is the deep and essential [G-dly] revelation from a supra-rational level that comes as a result of a logic-based worship of G-d. This is a supernal inspiration that comes as a result of and after an earthly inspiration in the form of a logic-based worship of G-d.[218]

The second type is an unprovoked supernal inspiration that [stems from a place that] an earthly inspiration cannot at all reach. A revelation of this sort occurred on Pesach; it was an unprovoked supernal inspiration, as in the verse, *I will be like dew to Israel.*[219]

The future redemption, the coming of the righteous redeemer, will therefore occur in Nissan; for Nissan is a time of unprovoked supernal inspiration,[220] when the treasure houses of dew are opened[221]—*I will be like dew to Israel.*[222]

---

218. This is a case where the supernal inspiration surpasses the earthly inspiration that triggered it. Nevertheless, it cannot be said that the supernal inspiration came *unprovoked.*

219. **Hosea 14:6, according to its interpretation in** *Likkutei Torah,* **discourse entitled** *Haazinu,* **ch. 6 [73b].**
Likkutei Torah ibid.: "'Dew' refers to an extremely lofty level that cannot be elicited through an earthly inspiration. For the deeds of mortals do not have the power to elicit this great love. Nevertheless, after the supernal inspiration caused by their deeds— which comes as 'rain'—then, of its own accord, and automatically, the level of 'dew' descends… It is for this reason that 'dew never ceases,' as our Sages tell us (*Taanit* 3a), since its source far transcends human deed…."
Rain represents Divine beneficence

that descends in response to human deed, just as rain is formed from moisture that has risen from the ground. Dew, by contrast, represents Divine beneficence that stems from a place where human deed cannot reach. Rain is reciprocal; dew, self-initiated.

Now, although "dew" descends only after man's spiritual service (which elicits "rain"), it is still considered as unprovoked inspiration initiated from above. Man's deeds do not *elicit* this inspiration, but rather ensure that the person not be an *impediment* to it. Indeed, every unprovoked supernal inspiration follows the perfection of man's deeds, since this inspiration must find a recipient that is as spiritually "whole" as it can be. As the *Zohar* states (III:90b): "G-d only rests in a place that is [spiritually] 'whole.'" See *Likkutei Torah, Shir Hashirim,* 23d ff.; *Sefer Ha-*

אִתְעֲרוּתָא דִּלְעֵילָּא הַבָּאָה עַל יְדֵי אִתְעֲרוּתָא דִלְתַתָּא, וּכְמוֹ
שֶׁעַל יְדֵי הָעֲבוֹדָה עַל פִּי טַעַם וָדַעַת מַמְשִׁיכִים גִּילוּי פְּנִימִי
וְעַצְמִי מִבְּחִינָה וּמַדְרֵיגָה שֶׁלְּמַעְלָה מִטַּעַם וָדַעַת, וְהוּא
הָאִתְעֲרוּתָא דִּלְעֵילָּא הַבָּאָה בְּסִבַּת וְאַחַר הָאִתְעֲרוּתָא דִּלְתַתָּא
בַּהֲעֲבוֹדָה דְּטַעַם וָדַעַת.

וְהַבּ' הִיא אִתְעֲרוּתָא דִּלְעֵילָּא מִצַּד עַצְמָהּ שֶׁאֵין אִתְעֲרוּתָא
דִלְתַתָּא מַגִּיעַ לְשָׁם כְּלָל, וְגִילוּי כָּזֶה הָיָה בְּפֶסַח, בְּחִינַת
אִתְעֲרוּתָא דִּלְעֵילָּא מִצַּד עַצְמָהּ, כְּמוֹ שֶׁכָּתוּב אֶהְיֶה כַטַּל[סב]
לְיִשְׂרָאֵל.

וְלָכֵן הִנֵּה הַגְּאוּלָה הָעֲתִידָה בִּיאַת הַגּוֹאֵל צֶדֶק תִּהְיֶה
בְּנִיסָן, שֶׁהוּא זְמַן הָאִתְעֲרוּתָא דִּלְעֵילָּא מִצַּד עַצְמָהּ, וּבוֹ
נִפְתָּחִין[סג] אוֹצְרוֹת טַל שֶׁהוּא אֶהְיֶה כַטַּל לְיִשְׂרָאֵל.

---

maamarim Melukat, vol. 6, p. 24.

220. In the Messianic Era, the Essence of G-d will be manifest. So although the redemption follows our Divine service during *galut* (exile), the revelation is nonetheless viewed as one that comes *unprovoked*, since no mortal act could ever elicit G-d's Essence (of its own accord). The Sages therefore maintain that the redemption will occur in Nissan, the time of unprovoked supernal inspiration.

221. *Pirkei d'Rabbi Eliezer*, ch. 32.
Pirkei d'Rabbi Eliezer, ibid.: "The night of Pesach arrived. Isaac called his older son [Esau] and said, 'My son, tonight the heavenly hosts are singing, tonight the treasure houses of dew are opened, today is [the day of] the blessing of dew. Prepare for me a tasty dish, and I will bless you while I

am yet alive.' The Divine Spirit responded, '*Do not eat the bread of the miserly!*' (Proverbs 23:6). Esau went to bring the food, but was withheld. Said Rebecca to Jacob, 'My son, tonight the treasure houses of dew are opened, tonight the heavenly hosts are singing. Prepare a tasty dish for your father, and he will eat. While he is yet alive he will bless you.'"

Pesach is thus the time when the Heavenly treasure houses of dew and blessing are open (which is why we recite the special prayer for dew on the first day of Pesach). In a more general sense, this is representative of the entire month of Nissan.

222. It is specifically in Nissan that G-d sends His unprovoked supernal inspiration—"dew"—to Israel. Nissan is therefore the most auspicious month for the future redemption.

9.

Another explanation for the advantage of Nissan over Tishrei:

The distinction of Tishrei is that it is the seventh and all sevenths are precious. But the distinction of the seventh is that it is seventh *to the first*. So even within the distinction of the seventh, the first is primary, since the advantage of the seventh is that is the seventh to the first. If so, even within this [distinction of the seventh], the first is primary.[223]

ABRAHAM AND MOSES

An example from the Patriarchs[224]: The seventh, the precious one, is Moses, peace be upon him, who is the seventh to Abraham. Abraham is the first and Moses is the seventh. So his distinction is the fact that he is seventh to the first.

Therefore, despite the magnitude of the greatness of Moses, whom G-d chose to be the first redeemer, we find written, *And [G-d] said, "Moses Moses," and [Moses] replied, "Here I am,"*[225] which the Midrash says is what is meant by the verse, *In the place of great ones do not stand*[226]—i.e., [Moses] should not equate himself with Abraham.[227]

For Abraham was the first to bring revelation of Divinity to the world through his work in publicizing the existence of

---

223. The very existence of a seventh presupposes a first, for there could not be a seventh had there not been a first. Furthermore, the very preciousness of the seventh is due to the fact that he actualizes and fully achieves the goal initiated by the first. It follows, then, that the first is primary, since without his initiative the seventh (and what the seventh accomplishes) would not exist. The Rebbe cites the example of Abraham and Moses. Abraham was the first to bring G-dliness into the world, and it was Moses, the seventh from Abraham, who actualized and fully

achieved what Abraham had begun, since it was Moses who brought G-d's presence into the world at Sinai (see following footnote).

224. *Vayikra Rabbah* 29:11. See above, footnote 204.

See also *Bati Legani 5710* (*Sefer Hamaamarim 5710*, p. 111), citing *Shir Hashirim Rabbah* 5:1: "At first, the *Shechinah* (Divine presence) was primarily in the lower world. But through the sin involving the Tree of Knowledge, the *Shechinah* ascended from the earth to the [first] heaven. Through the sins of successive genera-

ט.

וְעוֹד טַעַם בְּמַעֲלַת נִיסָן עַל תִּשְׁרֵי:

דְּהִנֵּה מַעֲלַת חֹדֶשׁ תִּשְׁרֵי שֶׁהוּא חֹדֶשׁ הַשְּׁבִיעִי וְכָל הַשְּׁבִיעִין חֲבִיבִין הִנֵּה מַעֲלָתוֹ שֶׁל הַשְּׁבִיעִי שֶׁהוּא שְׁבִיעִי לָרִאשׁוֹן, הֲרֵי הִנֵּה גַּם בְּמַעֲלַת הַשְּׁבִיעִי הָרִאשׁוֹן עִיקָּר, וְהַיְינוּ, דְּמַעֲלַת הַשְּׁבִיעִי הוּא שֶׁהוּא שְׁבִיעִי לָרִאשׁוֹן, אִם כֵּן הִנֵּה גַּם בָּזֶה הָעִיקָּר הוּא הָרִאשׁוֹן.

וּכְמוֹ בְּאָבוֹתⁱⁱ, הִנֵּה הַשְּׁבִיעִי הֶחָבִיב הוּא מֹשֶׁה רַבֵּינוּ עָלָיו הַשָּׁלוֹם, שֶׁהוּא שְׁבִיעִי לְאַבְרָהָם, דְּאַבְרָהָם הוּא הָרִאשׁוֹן וּמֹשֶׁה רַבֵּינוּ עָלָיו הַשָּׁלוֹם הוּא הַשְּׁבִיעִי, הֲרֵי שֶׁמַּעֲלָתוֹ הוּא שֶׁהוּא שְׁבִיעִי לָרִאשׁוֹן.

וְלָכֵן הִנֵּה בְּכָל עוֹצֶם גּוֹדֶל מַעֲלָתוֹ שֶׁל מֹשֶׁה רַבֵּינוּ עָלָיו הַשָּׁלוֹם, אֲשֶׁר אוֹתוֹ בָּחַר ה' לְגוֹאֵל רִאשׁוֹן, כְּתִיב וַיֹּאמֶר מֹשֶׁהⁱⁱ מֹשֶׁה וַיֹּאמֶר הִנֵּנִי, וְאִיתָא בְּמִדְרָשִׁיⁱⁱ, זֶהוּ שֶׁאָמַר הַכָּתוּב וּבִמְקוֹם גְּדוֹלִים אַל תַּעֲמוֹד, שֶׁלֹּא יִשְׁתַּוֶּוה עַצְמוֹ לְאַבְרָהָם אָבִינוּ עָלָיו הַשָּׁלוֹם.

דְּאַבְרָהָם אָבִינוּ עָלָיו הַשָּׁלוֹם הָיָה הָרִאשׁוֹן שֶׁהִמְשִׁיךְ גִּילּוּי

---

tions, the *Shechinah* ascended further and further, until after a seventh generation of sin it had ascended to the seventh heaven. At that point, seven righteous individuals arose and brought the *Shechinah* back to the lower world. Abraham merited and brought the *Shechinah* down from the seventh heaven to the sixth; Isaac brought it down from the sixth to the fifth, etc., until Moses, who was the seventh—and all sevenths are precious—brought it [back] down to the earth."

225. **Exodus 3:4.**

226. Proverbs 25:6.

227. *Devarim Rabbah* 2:7.
In responding to G-d's call, Moses uses the same phrase used by Abraham when he was called by G-d: *hineni*—"here I am," a phrase that connotes self-nullification and devotion. The Midrash says that G-d told Moses, *In the place of great ones do not stand*, meaning it was presumptuous of Moses to use that same phrase. This demonstrates the greatness of Abraham (the first) even with regard to Moses (the seventh).

G-d in the world.[228] He thereby brought light to the world, as the Midrash says: Before Abraham, the world operated in darkness. When Abraham came, the world began to shine.[229]

INSULAR RIGHTEOUSNESS

Before Abraham there were also great righteous men, such as Enoch, of whom it is written, *And Enoch walked with G-d.*[230] There was also Methuselah, in whose honor G-d postponed the Flood to a different time.[231] There was also Noah, of whom it is written that he was *a righteous man, perfect,* and that he *found favor in the eyes of G-d.*[232] Nevertheless, there was darkness in the world.

For although they were great righteous men, all [their focus] was self-directed. They did not do anything in the world [outside them].

Even Noah [who did rebuke his generation[233]]—not only did he not ask G-d to have mercy on his generation,[234] he did not even devote himself to find ways and plans to convince them to repent. In the 120 years during which he built the Ark,[235] he did not devote himself to the goal of ensuring that

---

228. On the verse (Genesis 21:33), *And there [Abraham] proclaimed the name of G-d*, the Talmud (*Sotah* 10a-b) relates how Abraham would share his theology with those he came in contact with:

Abraham lived in the desert, a place normally devoid of lavish provisions. Yet, his tent was always filled with the choicest foods and drinks—meat, wine and other delicacies. Whenever someone would pass by, Abraham would immediately invite them into his tent to enjoy the meal of their choice. When they had finished their meal and time came for them to take leave, they would begin to bless Abraham for his hospitality. To which he replied: "Was it of *my* food that you ate? It belonged to the

G-d of the world! Praise and bless the Creator of the World." In this way, Abraham would teach the people about G-d.

229. *Bereishit Rabbah* 2:3.

The Midrash interprets the verse (Genesis 1:2), *And the earth was unformed and desolate, and darkness covered the surface of the deep....*, as referring to the generations of Adam, Cain, Enosh and the generation of the Flood. Finally, G-d said, "How long shall the world operate in darkness?" *And G-d said: "Let there be light"* (ibid., v. 3)—this is Abraham, as it says (Isaiah 41:2), *Who inspired* (העיר) *[the one] from the east?* (referring to Abraham who came Canaan from Aram to the east). Do not

אֱלֹקוּת בָּעוֹלָם עַל יְדֵי עֲבוֹדָתוֹ לְפַרְסֵם אֱלֹקוּתוֹ יִתְבָּרֵךְ בָּעוֹלָם,
וּבָזֶה הֵאִיר אֶת הָעוֹלָם, וְכִדְאִיתָא בְּמִדְרָשׁ עַד אַבְרָהָם[סי] הָיָה
הָעוֹלָם מִתְנַהֵג בַּאֲפֵילָה, בָּא אַבְרָהָם הִתְחִיל לְהָאִיר.

דְּעַד אַבְרָהָם הָיָה גַם כֵּן צַדִּיקִים גְּדוֹלִים, כְּמוֹ חֲנוֹךְ
דִּכְתִיב בֵּיהּ וַיִּתְהַלֵּךְ חֲנוֹךְ[סח] אֶת הָאֱלֹקִים, וּמְתוּשֶׁלַח אֲשֶׁר
לִכְבוֹדוֹ[סט] דָּחָה הַקָּדוֹשׁ בָּרוּךְ הוּא אֶת הַמַּבּוּל לִזְמַן אַחֵר, וְנֹחַ
כְּתִיב בֵּיהּ צַדִּיק תָּמִים וּמָצָא חֵן[ע] בְּעֵינֵי ה', וּמִכָּל מָקוֹם הָיָה
אֲפֵילָה בָּעוֹלָם.

וְעִם הֱיוֹתָם צַדִּיקִים גְּדוֹלִים, אֲבָל הַכֹּל הָיָה בִּשְׁבִיל
עַצְמָם, וּבָעוֹלָם לֹא עָשׂוּ.

וַאֲפִילוּ נֹחַ, הִנֵּה לֹא זוֹ בִּלְבַד שֶׁלֹּא בִּיקֵּשׁ[עא] רַחֲמִים עַל
דוֹרוֹ, אֶלָּא אַף גַם לֹא נָתַן עַצְמוֹ לִמְצוֹא דְּרָכִים וְעֵצוֹת
שֶׁיִּפְעוֹל עֲלֵיהֶם לַעֲשׂוֹת תְּשׁוּבָה, וּבְמֵאָה וְעֶשְׂרִים שָׁנָה שֶׁבָּנָה
אֶת הַתֵּיבָה הִנֵּה לֹא נָתַן עַצְמוֹ עַל זֶה אֲשֶׁר תּוֹכַחְתּוֹ

---

read העיר, *inspired*, but האיר, *il-luminated*. The verse thus reads: *Who illuminated from the east?*—indicating that Abraham began to illuminate the world with the light of G-dliness.

230. Genesis 5:24.

231. *Sanhedrin* 108b.
G-d told Noah that after seven days He would bring the Flood (Genesis 7:4). The verse then states (v. 10): *And it came to pass after the seven-day period that the waters of the Flood were upon the earth.* The Talmud (ibid.) comments: "What is the nature of this *seven-day period*? Rav explained, these were the [seven] days of mourning for Methuselah [who had just died]."

232. Genesis 6:8-9.

233. See *Sanherdrin* 108a.: "Noah, the righteous one, rebuked them and told them, 'Repent.'"

234. *Zohar* I:106a. See also ibid. 67b ff.; ibid. 254b, III:14b ff.
The *Zohar* explains that the Flood is referred to in Scripture as *The waters of Noah* (Isaiah 54:9)—a phrase that seems to attribute the Flood's responsibility to Noah—since he did not beseech G-d to have mercy on the world.

235. See *Rashi* on Genesis 6:3 and 6:14.

his rebuke and warnings should influence his generation and inspire them to repentance, with regret for the past and good resolutions for the future—something that Abraham and Moses gave their lives to do.[236]

Instead, if someone *asked him* why he was building the Ark, he would tell him that G-d is going to bring a flood upon the earth to wipe out man because of the wickedness of his deeds.[237] Not only did he not teach them to know G-d, to explain to them and help them understand that He created the world out of nothingness and that He, the One and Only Creator, conducts [the affairs of] the world and keeps watch over every single creation with particular attention (*hashgacha pratit*), this being its life-force, and He arranges for all of its needs—not only did Noah not teach them [this], he did not even rebuke them[238] nor did he ask G-d to have mercy on them.

This is what it means that [before Abraham] the world operated in darkness. Although there were people that were completely righteous, the *world* remained dark.[239] But when Abraham came along, the world began to shine, as it says, *Who inspired [the one] from the east, [at whose every footstep] righteousness [attended]?*[240]—do not read it העיר (*inspired*) but האיר (*illuminated*), with an *alef.*[241]

---

236. Noah's ambivalence stands in stark contrast with the behavior of Abraham and Moses in similar circumstances. When G-d told Abraham of the imminent destruction of Sodom and its neighboring cities, Abraham immediately implored G-d to reconsider, praying that He spare any one of the condemned cities if there were but ten righteous people in their midst (see Genesis 18:20-33). And Moses implored G-d to forgive the Children of Israel after the sin of the Golden Calf, going so far as asking G-d to remove his (Moses') name from the entire Torah if G-d would

not forgive them (Exodus 32:32). See *Zohar*, ibid.

237. *Sanhedrin* **ibid.**

238. Although our Sages tell us that Noah did indeed rebuke the people (see above, footnote 233), he did so only to discharge his obligation to rebuke. He was not truly concerned as to whether his rebuke would be effective. Thus, Noah did not rebuke them *wholeheartedly* (see *Likkutei Sichot*, vol. 15, pp. 40-41).

239. Since none of the righteous men

וְהִתְרָאוֹתָיו יִפְעֲלוּ עֲלֵיהֶם לְעוֹרְרָם לִתְשׁוּבָה, בַּחֲרָטָה עַל הֶעָבַר וּבְקַבָּלָה טוֹבָה עַל לְהַבָּא, כְּמוֹ שֶׁעָשׂוּ אַבְרָהָם וּמֹשֶׁה שֶׁמָּסְרוּ נַפְשָׁם עַל זֶה.

אֶלָּא אִם מִי שֶׁהוּא‎ᵛ שָׁאַל אוֹתוֹ לָמָה הוּא בּוֹנֶה אֶת הַתֵּיבָה, הִגִּיד לוֹ שֶׁעָתִיד הַקָּדוֹשׁ בָּרוּךְ הוּא לְהָבִיא מַבּוּל עַל הָאָרֶץ לִמְחוֹת אֶת הָאָדָם מִפְּנֵי רוֹעַ מַעַלְלֵיהֶם, וְעִם זֶה, הִנֵּה לֹא זוֹ בִּלְבַד שֶׁלֹּא לִימֵּד אוֹתָם לָדַעַת אֶת ה‎/, לַהֲבִינָם וּלְהַסְבִּירָם שֶׁהוּא יִתְבָּרֵךְ בָּרָא אֶת הָעוֹלָם מְלֹא דָבָר לְדָבָר, וְהוּא יִתְבָּרֵךְ בּוֹרֵא יָחִיד מַנְהִיג אֶת הָעוֹלָם וּמַשְׁגִּיחַ עַל כָּל נִבְרָא וְנִבְרָא בְּהַשְׁגָּחָה פְּרָטִית, אֲשֶׁר זֶהוּ חַיּוּתוֹ, וּמַזְמִין לוֹ כָּל צְרָכָיו, הִנֵּה לֹא זוֹ בִּלְבַד אֲשֶׁר לֹא לִימֵּד אוֹתָם, אֶלָּא אַף גַּם לֹא הוֹכִיחַ אוֹתָם וְלֹא בִקֵּשׁ עֲלֵיהֶם רַחֲמִים.

וְזֶהוּ שֶׁהָעוֹלָם הָיָה מְשַׁמֵּשׁ בַּאֲפֵילָה, דְּהַגַם שֶׁהָיוּ צַדִּיקִים גְּמוּרִים, אֲבָל בָּעוֹלָם הָיָה אֲפֵילָה, וּמִכֵּיוָן שֶׁבָּא‎ᵛ אַבְרָהָם הִתְחִיל לְהָאִיר, וּכְמוֹ שֶׁכָּתוּב מִי הֵעִיר מִמִּזְרָח צֶדֶק, אַל תִּקְרֵי הֵעִיר אֶלָּא הֵאִיר בָּא‎/.

---

who lived before Abraham were concerned with introducing society to the One G-d and influencing the people to act in accordance with His will, the world remained spiritually "dark."

240. Isaiah 41:2. This verse refers to Abraham, who hailed from Aram, which lies to the east of Canaan. Wherever Abraham went, he exhorted the populace to righteousness—to abandon the false gods and believe in the One true G-d (*Metzudot David* ad loc.) Alternatively, the righteousness performed by Abraham accompanied him wherever he went (*Rashi* ad loc.)

241. *Bereishit Rabbah* 2:3.

In the simple meaning of the verse, G-d is asking a rhetorical question: *Who inspired* (העיר) *[the one] from the east [Abraham]?*—the answer being G-d Himself. The Midrash, however, reads the verse as *Who illuminated* (האיר) *from the east?*—the answer being Abraham, who began to illuminate the world with G-dliness.

The discourse proceeds to combine both interpretations of the word *hei'ir*, rendering the verse as follows: *Who brought inspiration and illumination from the east?* Abraham, who *inspired* his generation, and *illuminated* their minds with the concept of Monotheism.

Now, it is known that the intention of all "do not reads" is that both interpretations are included in the given word.[242] [So in this case, the word *hei'ir* connotes that] Abraham's work included two things: 1) He *inspired* the people of his generation so that they would not err and follow the graven images and idols; 2) he *illuminated* the eyes of their minds to explain to them and help them understand the concept of Creation, that He is the One and Only Creator. This he did with self-sacrifice, not for his own benefit.

ABRAHAM AND R. AKIVA

This is the difference between the self-sacrifice of [Abraham and that of] R. Akiva, who said, "When will [the opportunity for actual self-sacrifice] come to my hands, so that I may fulfill it?"[243] R. Akiva desired the experience of self-sacrifice for his own benefit, because of the great significance of self-sacrifice. The self-sacrifice of Abraham, by contrast, was applied only to publicizing the existence of G-d in the world itself.[244]

R. Akiva therefore derived pleasure from his pain, since it was through [his suffering] that his desire to sacrifice his life for G-d was fulfilled. Abraham, on the other hand, was pained by the fact that he was locked up in prison,[245] since he was unable to carry on with his work of publicizing G-dliness in the world.[246]

---

242. *Sefer Halichot Eli*, et al., cited in the books of Talmudic principles. Our Sages often explain a given verse or word in a manner that differs from its literal meaning, by exchanging certain vowels or letters, thus giving it another connotation. When that happens, both interpretations—the literal and non-literal—stand together.

243. *Berachot* 61b.
R. Akiva was arrested by the Romans for teaching Torah and was sentenced to death. The Talmud (ibid.)

relates that when they were about to execute him, it was the time for the recitation of the *Shema*. They were scraping his flesh with iron combs and he was accepting upon himself the yoke of Heaven (i.e., reading the *Shema*—Rashi). His students exclaimed: "Our teacher, even to this extent?" He replied: "All my days I was distressed over this verse (Deuteronomy 6:5), *[Love G-d] with all your soul*, which means even if He takes your soul. I said, 'When will [the opportunity for actual self-

וְיָדוּעַ דְּכָל אַל תִּקְרֵי הַכַּוָּנָה™ שֶׁכּוֹלֵל ב' הַפֵּירוּשִׁים, דְּאַבְרָהָם אָבִינוּ עָלָיו הַשָּׁלוֹם הָיְתָה עֲבוֹדָתוֹ בְּב' הָעִנְיָנִים, שֶׁהֵעִיר אֶת אַנְשֵׁי דוֹרוֹ שֶׁלֹּא יִטְעוּ אַחֲרֵי הַפְּסִילִים וְהַגִּלּוּלִים, וְהֵאִיר עֵינֵי שִׂכְלָם לַהֲבִינָם וּלְהַסְבִּירָם עִנְיַן הַבְּרִיאָה שֶׁהוּא יִתְבָּרֵךְ בּוֹרֵא יָחִיד, וַעֲבוֹדָתוֹ זֹאת עָשָׂה בִּמְסִירַת נֶפֶשׁ, וְשֶׁלֹּא לְטוֹבַת עַצְמוֹ.

דְּזֶהוּ הַהֶפְרֵשׁ בֵּין הַמְסִירַת נֶפֶשׁ דְּרַבִּי עֲקִיבָא™, שֶׁאָמַר מָתַי יָבֹא לְיָדִי וַאֲקַיְּימֶנּוּ, שֶׁחָפֵץ בִּמְסִירַת נֶפֶשׁ לְטוֹבַת עַצְמוֹ מִצַּד גּוֹדֶל הָעִנְיָן שֶׁבְּמְסִירַת נֶפֶשׁ, וְאַבְרָהָם אָבִינוּ עָלָיו הַשָּׁלוֹם הַמְסִירַת נֶפֶשׁ שֶׁלּוֹ הָיָה רַק עַל עִנְיַן פִּרְסוּם אֱלֹקוּת בָּעוֹלָם בְּעַצְמוֹ.

לָכֵן הִנֵּה רַבִּי עֲקִיבָא הָיָה לוֹ עֹנֶג בְּהַצַּעַר שֶׁלּוֹ, כִּי בָּזֶה נִתְמַלֵּא מְבוּקָשׁוֹ לִמְסוֹר נַפְשׁוֹ עַל אֱלֹקוּת, וְאַבְרָהָם אָבִינוּ עָלָיו הַשָּׁלוֹם הָיָה לוֹ צַעַר מִזֶּה שֶׁנֶּחְבַּשׁ בְּבֵית הָאֲסוּרִים™, וְהַצַּעַר הָיָה לְפִי שֶׁנִּתְבַּטֵּל מֵעֲבוֹדָתוֹ לְפַרְסֵם אֱלֹקוּתוֹ יִתְבָּרֵךְ בָּעוֹלָם.

---

sacrifice] come to my hands, so that I may fulfill it?' And now that it has indeed come to my hands, shall I not fulfill it?"

244. Abraham's motives for his self-sacrifice were pure, and were not at all self-serving; i.e., his self-sacrifice was for publicizing G-dliness in the world, not for his own spiritual advancement.

245. *Bava Batra* 91a; *Pirkei d'Rabbi Eliezer* 26.

The Talmud (ibid.) states that Abraham was imprisoned for ten years. *Rashbam* (ad loc.) comments

that he was imprisoned by King Nimrod. He also cites an *Aggadah* to the effect that Abraham was imprisoned by his own father, Terah, for destroying the latter's idols.

246. From the third chapter of *Bati Legani 5711*, the inaugural discourse delivered by Rabbi Yosef Yitzchak's son-in-law and successor, Rabbi Menachem Mendel Schneerson, the seventh Rebbe of the Chabad-Lubavitch dynasty, on the first anniversary of the former's passing:

"My father-in-law explained (at the beginning of his arrival to America) that even in the preciousness of the

And because Abraham was the first to bring Divine revelation to the world, Moses, who is the seventh from Abraham, is precious.

The same is true of Tishrei, which is the seventh from Nissan. Nissan [the first month] is therefore the month of redemption.[247]

BEYOND NATURE WITHIN NATURE

Hence, *This month is for you the first of months*—since Nissan is the month of redemption.[248] Yet, *it is, for you, the first of the months of the year*, since even in *the months of the year*, which refers to the Divine radiance that is elicited into the world within the garments of nature—*it is, for you, the first*:

To the souls of Israel, even in *the months of the year*, which are the world's natural garments, it will be *this month*, i.e., the month of redemption, which transcends nature. In other words, Divinity that transcends nature will be sensed even within nature.[249]

---

seventh the virtue of the first is apparent, since being seventh means that he is seventh to the first. He then explained the virtue of the first one, who is Abraham, because of his work and that his work was done with self-sacrifice. He does not suffice with that and adds (although it does not seem to be relevant to the matter at hand) that the manner of his self-sacrifice was that he did not *seek* self-sacrifice. And this is the difference between the self-sacrifice of Abraham and that of R. Akiva. The latter's was such that he sought self-sacrifice—'when will it come to my hands, so that I may fulfill it.' The self-sacrifice of Abraham, by contrast, was incidental. Abraham knew that his primary service was, *And there he proclaimed the name of G-d, G-d of the world* (Genesis 21:33)—'do

not read it as *he proclaimed*, but as *he caused others to proclaim*' (*Sotah* 10a-b). If this required self-sacrifice—incidentally—he was prepared to undergo it. His greatness and work was so great that it gave merit to Moses to receive the Torah, since all sevenths are precious because he is the seventh after the first. G-d therefore said to Moses, *In the place of great ones do not stand* (Proverbs 25:6).

"Now, although the preciousness of the seventh is great, and it does not come to him through his own volition or effort—it comes complete and ready from birth—nevertheless, one cannot say of it, *It is beyond me* (Deuteronomy 30:11) and is appropriate only for select individuals. Rather... all of Israel can attain the level of being a vessel for the Holy Spirit, and

וְלִהְיוֹתוֹ הָרִאשׁוֹן שֶׁהִמְשִׁיךְ גִּילּוּי אֱלֹקוּת בָּעוֹלָם, הִנֵּה מֹשֶׁה שֶׁהָיָה שְׁבִיעִי לְאַבְרָהָם הוּא חָבִיב.

אֲשֶׁר כֵּן הוּא גַּם בְּתִשְׁרֵי שֶׁהוּא שְׁבִיעִי לְנִיסָן, לָכֵן הִנֵּה נִיסָן הוּא חֹדֶשׁ הַגְּאוּלָה.

וְזֶהוּ הַחֹדֶשׁ הַזֶּה לָכֶם רֹאשׁ חֳדָשִׁים, לִהְיוֹת נִיסָן הוּא זְמַן הַגְּאוּלָה. וְרִאשׁוֹן הוּא לָכֶם לְחָדְשֵׁי הַשָּׁנָה, דְּגַם בְּחָדְשֵׁי הַשָּׁנָה, שֶׁהוּא הֶאָרָה הָאֱלֹקִית שֶׁנִּמְשְׁכָה בָּעוֹלָם בִּלְבוּשֵׁי הַטֶּבַע, הִנֵּה רִאשׁוֹן הוּא לָכֶם.

דְּבְנִשְׁמוֹת יִשְׂרָאֵל, הִנֵּה גַּם בְּחָדְשֵׁי הַשָּׁנָה, שֶׁהֵם לְבוּשֵׁי הַטֶּבַע דְּעוֹלָם, יִהְיֶה הַחֹדֶשׁ הַזֶּה, שֶׁהוּא הַחֹדֶשׁ שֶׁל גְּאוּלָה שֶׁהוּא לְמַעְלָה מֵהַטֶּבַע. וְהַיְינוּ, שֶׁגַּם בְּטֶבַע יִהְיֶה נִרְגָּשׁ הָאֱלֹקוּת הַבִּלְתִּי מִתְלַבֵּשׁ בְּטֶבַע.

---- ◆►◄◆ ----

all of Israel must say, 'When will my deeds reach those of my Patriarchs, Abraham, Isaac and Jacob' (*Tanna d'Vei Eliyahu Rabbah*, ch. 25). Nevertheless, one need not fool oneself. One must know that *in the place of the great ones do not stand*. The very greatness of the seventh is that he is seventh to the first—that he is capable of accomplishing the work and mission of the first, which is 'do not read it as *he proclaimed*, but as *he caused others to proclaim*.'

"And this is the preciousness of the seventh, that he is the one that elicits the Divine presence. Furthermore, he elicits the primary aspect of the Divine presence; and furthermore, he does so in the lowest realms" (*Sefer Hamaamarim Melukat*, vol. 1, p. 5).

247. Although Tishrei is precious by virtue of its being seventh, it greatness is nonetheless due to the *first*, the month of Nissan. That is why Nissan is ultimately the month of redemption.

248. As we explained before, *months* connotes revelation and redemption. The *first of months*, therefore, is Nissan, "the month of redemption."

249. The Jew is undaunted by the obscuring veil of physicality, for the soul—a literal piece of G-d (*Tanya*, ch. 2)—remains forever bound with its source in a manner that transcends the restrictions of the corporeal. Therefore, even within *the months of the year*, nature, the Jew senses the supernatural, transcendent force of G-d—*this month*.

HEBREW NOTES

HEBREW NOTES

‫א. החודש הזה: שמות יב, ב.‬

‫ב. משבחר הקב״ה: שמות רבה פט״ו, יא.‬

‫ג. בר״ה בטלה: ר״ה יא, א.‬

‫ד. פלוגתא בגמרא: ר״ה שם.‬

‫ה. ובמד״ר הכריעו: שמ״ר פט״ו, יא.‬

‫ו. ויקהלו אל המלך: מלכים א ח, ב.‬

‫ז. בכ״ה באלול נבה״ע: ויקרא רבה ר״פ כט. פסיקתא בחדש השביעי. — והא‬
‫דתניא בתשרי נבה״ע, גמר ברייתו קאמרינן (ר״ן בר״ה טז, א).‬

‫ח. והיו לאותות: בראשית א, יד. וצע״ק הראי׳.‬

‫ט. כמאן מצלינן: ראה ר״ה כז, א ויק״ר ופסיקתא שם.‬

‫י. אנכי ה׳: שמות כ, ב.‬

‫יא. הי׳ אבן: שמות רבה סוף פ״ח. מכילתא שמות יז, ו.‬

‫יב. או עץ: במדבר רבה סוף פי״ח. זוהר ח״ב קטו, א. ילקוט ראובני פ׳ וארא.‬
‫וראה פרקי דר״א פ״מ.‬

‫יג. מי שאמר לשמן: תענית כה, א (כגירסת העין יעקב)‬

‫יד. בעשרה מאמרות: אבות פ״ה מ״א.‬

‫טו. בח״ב בתניא: פ״א ופרק יב.‬

‫טז. בראשית ברא: בראשית א, א.‬

‫יז. מן הארץ: חגיגה יג, א.‬

‫יח. ומלאך בשליש: בראשית רבה פס״ח, יב — בשינוי לשון.‬

‫יט. המלאך הוא שליש העולם: ב״ר שם. חולין צא, ב.‬

‫כ. או שהעולם: מובא פי׳ זה גם בד״ה וראיתי אני דשנת תרס״ב. ולע״ע לא‬
‫ידעתי מקורו.‬

‫כא. דשרפים . . ואופנים: חולין צב, א.‬

‫כב. וכמצבי׳ עביד: דניאל ד, לב.‬

‫כג. דמיכאל עבודתו: ראה לקו״ת במדבר ד״ה וספרתם וביאורו ועוד.‬

‫כד. מלכותך מלכות: תהלים קמה, יג.‬

‫כה. יחיו חי: ברכת ברוך שאמר.‬

‫כו. וכשהרתיח: ב״מ פו, ב. וראה ב״ר פמ״ח, ח.‬

‫כז. הי׳ בצער: רש״י וירא.‬

‫כח. דידוע שיש: ראה ד״ה ואברהם זקן, תרס״ו. ד״ה ביום השמע״צ, תרפ״ט.‬

‫כט. בהמה רבה שבנינוה: סוף יונה.‬

‫ל. זכור רחמיך: תהלים כה, ו.‬

‫לא. חצוניות שבעליון: ראה ע״ח שער יד פ״ט. לקו״ת פ׳ שלח ד״ה ענין‬
‫הנסכים.‬

‫לב. אין מלך: עמק המלך שער שעשועי המלך רפ״א. ס׳ החיים פ׳ גאולה‬
‫פ״ב. בחיי וישב לח, ל. תניא ח״ב פ״ז.‬

לג. אמר הקב״ה: ר״ה לד, ב.

לד. אדה״ר שקבל: פרקי דר״א פי״א.

לה. כי ששת: שמות כ, יא ועפמ״ש בזהר (ח״ב פט, סע״ב) שמדבר בששה מדות.

לו. מלך שמו: פיוט אדון עולם.

לז. שבו ועל ידו: ראה לקו״ת ד״ה את שבתותי ס״ב. לקמן ד״ה בעצם היום.

לח. ידוע שזהו: ראה לקו״ת ביאור לד״ה אלה מסעי (השלישי).

לט. שזהו כללות: עיי״ש בלקו״ת.

מ. אשר מלך: פיוט אדון עולם.

מא. מל׳ בוקעת: עץ חיים שער סדר אבי״ע רפ״ו ושער דרושי אבי״ע פ״א. משנת חסידים מס׳ הבריאה ספ״א ורפ״ב. ועוד.

מב. כי נשגב: תהלים קמח, י״ג.

מג. הס געה״ע וגעה״ת: לקו״ת במדבר סוף הביאור לד״ה בשעה שהקדימו.

מד. בדבר ה׳: תהלים לג, ו.

מה. ואתה מחי׳: נחמי׳ ט, ו.

מו. כבוד מלכותך: תהלים קמה, יא.

מז. ואני תפלה וקאי על בחי׳ מל׳: תהלים קט, ד ועפמ״ש בזוהר ח״ג מט, ב.

מח. אנכי הוא בחי׳ כתר: ראה לקו״ת ד״ה לבאר כו׳ ונקדשתי ס״ה.

מט. כשל בעוני: תהלים לא, יא.

נ. ועברתי בארץ: שמות יב, יב.

נא. עד שנגלה: הגדה של פסח.

נב. עד שלא נבה״ע: פרקי דר״א פ״ג — יש שם גירסאות אחרות, אבל ראה דיוק גירסא זו דוקא בהקדמת השל״ה בתחלתה.

נג. אבל נשמות עלו: ראה לעיל ד״ה כי עמך מקור ס״ז.

נד. די״ב חדשי: ראה זח״ג רעז, סע״ב. פרדס שער כא פרק ו־ז.

נה. דכל השביעין חביבין: ויקרא רבה פכ״ט, יא.

נו. כימי צאתך: מיכה ז, טו.

נז. ניסן הוא חסד ותשרי גבורה: ראה זח״ב (קפו, א): החדש הזה לכם כו׳ כסדר דאתווין אביב כו׳ ירחא שביעאה דילי איהו מסופא דאתוון. ושם (נא, ב): אתוון כו׳ כסדרן כו׳ אשתכחו בחסד כו׳ למפרע כו׳ משתכחו בגבורה. — ולהעיר מל״ת להאריז״ל פ׳ ויצא ד״ה ענין הז׳ כוכבי לכת: מניסן ועד אלול כו׳ זכרום כו׳ חג״ת נה״י כו׳ ומתשרי כו׳ גבורות גשמים או״ח נוקבא (וצ״ע ממ״ש להיפך: בטעמי המצות פ׳ בא — הובא בעטרת ראש בתחלת הדרוש לעשי״ת, — בפע״ח שער ר״ה פ״ד, בשער הכוונות ענין ר״ה ד״א, בנהר שלום — בסוף ע״ח דפוס ורשא — בסופו). וראה קהלת יעקב מע׳ יב חדשים.

נח. דלכן אין אומרים: שו״ע רבנו הזקן סי׳ תקפ״ב ס״י. וצע״ק.

נט. שענינה תשובה: ראה לקמן ד״ה שופר של ר״ה.

ס. מצה זו: הגדה של פסח.

סא. דודי לי: שה״ש ב, טז. ראה לקמן ד״ה אני לדודי.

סב. אהי׳ כטל: הושע יד, ו. ועפמ״ש בלקו״ת ד״ה האזינו ס״ו.

סג. ובו נפתחין: פרקי דר״א פל״ב.

סד. וכמו באבות: ויקרא רבה פכ״ט, יא.

סה. ויאמר משה: שמות ג, ד.

סו. ואיתא במדרש: דברים רבה פ״ב, ז.

סז. עד אברהם: בראשית רבה פ״ב, ג.

סח. ויתהלך חנוך: בראשית ה, כד.

סט. אשר לכבודו: סנהדרין קח, ב.

ע. צדיק תמים ומצא חן: בראשית ו, ט; ו, ח.

עא. שלא ביקש: זוהר ח״א קו, א.

עב. אם מי שהוא: סנהדרין שם.

עג. ומכיון שבא: בראשית רבה פ״ב, ג.

עד. אל תקרי הכוונה: ס׳ הליכות אלי ועוד והובא בספרי כללי הש״ס.

עה. המס״נ דרע״ק: ברכות סא, ב.

עו. שנחבש בבית האסורים: בבא בתרא צא, א. פדר״א פכ״ו.

APPENDICES

❖

THE LETTERS OF CREATION

❖

CREATION VS. SPLITTING OF THE SEA

❖

MALCHUT AND THE OTHER SEFIROT

APPENDIX I

THE LETTERS OF CREATION
Shaar Hayichud Veha'emunah, Chapters 1 and 12

Chapter 1

Know this day and take it unto your heart that G-d is the [mighty and just] L-rd in the heavens above and upon the earth below; there is none other.[1]

This requires explanation. For would it [really] occur to you that there is a god dwelling in the waters beneath the earth, to the point that it is necessary to caution so strongly [and negate this thought by stating that one should] *take it unto your heart* [and come to the realization that this is indeed not so]?

It is written: *Forever, O G-d, Your word stands firm in the heavens.*[2] The Baal Shem Tov, of blessed memory, has explained [this concept at length, and made it widely known[3] that this means] that *Your word* which you uttered, i.e., *Let there be a firmament in the midst of the waters...,*[4] these very words and letters [through which the heavens were created] stand firmly forever within the firmament of heaven and are forever clothed within all the heavens to give them life,[5] as it is written, *The word of our L-rd shall stand firm forever,*[6] and [it is likewise written] *His words live and stand firm forever....*[7]

For if the [creative] letters were to depart [even] for an in-

---

1. Deuteronomy 4:39.

This verse continues the idea of an earlier verse (v. 35), which begins with the phrase אתה הראת (*You have been shown...*), and which refers to the time at which the Torah was given. At that time *G-d spoke to you...* (v. 12) with a warning against worshiping any of the components of the created universe: *Lest you become corrupt* (v. 16) and worship creatures of the lowest level, i.e., *any fish in* *the water below the earth* (v. 18), or of the highest level, i.e., *lest you raise your eyes heavenward....* (v. 19).

The verse, if understood simplistically, seems to declare that there are no other gods dwelling in heaven or earth.

2. Psalms 119:89.

3. **As mentioned in *Likkutei Torah*, beginning of *Parshat Acharei* [25c],**

הוֹסָפָה א

שַׁעַר הַיִּחוּד וְהָאֱמוּנָה, פְּרָקִים א וי"ב

פֶּרֶק א

וְיָדַעְתָּ הַיּוֹם וַהֲשֵׁבֹתָ אֶל לְבָבֶךָ כִּי ה' הוּא הָאֱלֹהִים בַּשָּׁמַיִם מִמַּעַל וְעַל הָאָרֶץ מִתָּחַת, אֵין עוֹד.

וְצָרִיךְ לְהָבִין, וְכִי תַעֲלֶה עַל דַּעְתְּךָ שֶׁיֵּשׁ אֱלֹהִים נִשְׁרֶה בַּמַּיִם מִתַּחַת לָאָרֶץ, שֶׁצָּרִיךְ לְהַזְהִיר כָּל כַּךְ וַהֲשֵׁבֹתָ אֶל לְבָבֶךָ.

הִנֵּה כְּתִיב לְעוֹלָם ה' דְּבָרְךָ נִצָּב בַּשָּׁמָיִם, וּפֵירֵשׁ הַבַּעַל שֵׁם טוֹב זִכְרוֹנוֹ לִבְרָכָה, כִּי דְּבָרְךָ שֶׁאָמַרְתָּ יְהִי רָקִיעַ בְּתוֹךְ הַמַּיִם וְגוֹ', תֵּיבוֹת וְאוֹתִיּוֹת אֵלּוּ הֵן נִצָּבוֹת וְעוֹמְדוֹת לְעוֹלָם בְּתוֹךְ רְקִיעַ הַשָּׁמַיִם, וּמְלוּבָּשׁוֹת בְּתוֹךְ כָּל הָרְקִיעִים לְעוֹלָם לְהַחֲיוֹתָם, כְּדִכְתִיב וּדְבַר אֱלֹהֵינוּ יָקוּם לְעוֹלָם, וּדְבָרָיו חַיִּים וְקַיָּימִים לָעַד כו'.

כִּי אִילּוּ הָיוּ הָאוֹתִיּוֹת מִסְתַּלְּקוֹת כְּרֶגַע חַס וְשָׁלוֹם

---

the germ of this concept is to be found in *Midrash Tanchuma* (on this verse).

4. Genesis 1:6.

5. **The fact that these words were uttered thousands of years ago presents no problem**—as Rabbi Schneur Zalman now continues to explain.

6. Isaiah 40:8.

7. Liturgy, Morning Prayer.

This refers not only to those creations such as the heavenly firmament which enjoy a permanent existence, but also to those creatures which perish as individuals, with only their species continuing to exist. In all instances, the Divine life-force which created a particular creature must constantly be vested within it, incessantly creating and vivifying it anew, just as it ceaselessly recreates the heavenly firmament, as shall soon be explained.

stant, G-d forbid, and return to their source,[8] all the heavens would become naught and absolute nothingness, and it would be as though they had never existed at all, exactly as before the utterance, *Let there be a firmament.*[9]

And so it is with all created things, in all the upper and lower worlds, and even this physical earth and the realm of the completely inanimate.[10] If the letters of the "ten utterances" by which the earth was created during the Six Days of Creation were to depart from it [but] for an instant, G-d forbid, it would revert to naught and absolute nothingness, exactly as before the Six Days of Creation.

This thought was expressed by the Arizal,[11] [when he said] that even within [that which appears to be] utterly inanimate matter, such as stones or earth or water, there is a soul and spiritual life-force. That is, [i.e., although they evince no demonstrable form of animation,] within them are [nevertheless] clothed the letters of speech from the "ten utterances" which give life and existence to inanimate matter, enabling it to come into being out of the naught and nothingness that preceded the Six Days of Creation.[12]

Now, although the name אבן (stone) is not mentioned in the "ten utterances" recorded in the Torah,[13] nevertheless, life-force flows to the stone [from the "ten utterances"] by means of combinations and substitutions of [their] letters,[14] which are transposed in the "two hundred and thirty-one gates," either in direct or reverse order,[15] as is explained in *Sefer Yet-*

---

8. That source being the degree of G-dliness from whence they emanate.

9. Before that Divine utterance the firmament did not exist at all. Were the letters that constitute the Divine utterance to depart from the firmament, it would revert to the state of never having existed at all.
Rabbi Schneur Zalman now concludes that this is true not only of the firmament, but of all created beings.

10. Even immobile beings that show no signs of animation or spirituality—not even the degree of animation observed in the process of growth in the vegetative world—even this extremely low life-form constantly harbors within it the Divine life-force that brought it into being.

11. See also *Eitz Chaim, Shaar* **50** (**ch. 2, 10**).

וְחוֹזְרוֹת לִמְקוֹרָן, הָיוּ כָּל הַשָּׁמַיִם אַיִן וְאֶפֶס מַמָּשׁ, וְהָיוּ
כְּלֹא הָיוּ כְּלָל, וּכְמוֹ קוֹדֶם מַאֲמַר יְהִי רָקִיעַ כו' מַמָּשׁ.

וְכֵן בְּכָל הַבְּרוּאִים שֶׁבְּכָל הָעוֹלָמוֹת עֶלְיוֹנִים
וְתַחְתּוֹנִים, וַאֲפִילוּ אֶרֶץ הַלֵּזוּ הַגַּשְׁמִית וּבְחִינַת דּוֹמֵם מַמָּשׁ,
אִילוּ הָיוּ מִסְתַּלְּקוֹת מִמֶּנָּה כְּרֶגַע חַס וְשָׁלוֹם הָאוֹתִיּוֹת
מֵעֲשָׂרָה מַאֲמָרוֹת שֶׁבָּהֶן נִבְרֵאת הָאָרֶץ בְּשֵׁשֶׁת יְמֵי בְרֵאשִׁית,
הָיְתָה חוֹזֶרֶת לְאַיִן וְאֶפֶס מַמָּשׁ, כְּמוֹ לִפְנֵי שֵׁשֶׁת יְמֵי
בְרֵאשִׁית מַמָּשׁ.

וְזֶהוּ שֶׁכָּתַב הָאֲרִ"י זַ"ל שֶׁגַּם בְּדוֹמֵם מַמָּשׁ, כְּמוֹ אֲבָנִים
וְעָפָר וּמַיִם, יֵשׁ בְּחִינַת נֶפֶשׁ וְחַיּוּת רוּחָנִית, דְּהַיְינוּ, בְּחִינַת
הִתְלַבְּשׁוּת אוֹתִיּוֹת הַדִּבּוּר מֵעֲשָׂרָה מַאֲמָרוֹת הַמְּחַיּוֹת
וּמְהַוּוֹת אֶת הַדּוֹמֵם, לִהְיוֹת יֵשׁ מֵאַיִן וְאֶפֶס שֶׁלִּפְנֵי שֵׁשֶׁת
יְמֵי בְרֵאשִׁית.

וְאַף שֶׁלֹּא הוּזְכַּר שֵׁם אֶבֶן בַּעֲשָׂרָה מַאֲמָרוֹת שֶׁבַּתּוֹרָה,
אַף עַל פִּי כֵן, נִמְשָׁךְ חַיּוּת לָאֶבֶן עַל יְדֵי צֵירוּפִים וְחִילוּפֵי
אוֹתִיּוֹת הַמִּתְגַּלְגְּלוֹת בְּרֵ"לֵא שְׁעָרִים פָּנִים וְאָחוֹר, כְּמוֹ

---

12. The "ten utterances" usher in-animate matter into a state of existence, in contrast to its former state of non-being, prior to the Six Days of Creation. Thus, the letters of the "ten utterances" which cause inanimate matter to be created are its soul and life-force.

13. I.e., how then can we say that letters of the "ten utterances" are clothed within a stone?

14. Whereby an *alef*, for example, may take the place of a *hey*, since both

letters are articulated by the same organ of speech, and so on.

15. Enumerated in detail in *Sefer Hapardes, Shaar Hatziruf*, ch. 5.
The twenty-two letters of the Hebrew alphabet in two-lettered combinations yield a total of 462 combinations. Of these, half are the exact reverse of the othesr half, e.g., *alef-bet, bet-alef*. Hence, there are 231 two-lettered combinations in direct order and the same number in reverse order.

zirah,[16] so that ultimately the combination of [letters that forms] the name אבן descends from the "ten utterances," and is derived from them—and this [combination of letters] is the life-force of the stone.

And so it is with all created things in the world.[17] The names [of all creatures] in the Holy Tongue are the very letters of speech which descend, degree by degree, from the "ten utterances" recorded in the Torah, by means of substitutions and transpositions of letters through the "two hundred and thirty-one gates," until they reach a particular created thing and become invested in it, thereby giving it life.

[This descent is necessary] because individual creatures, [unlike the more pervasive beings such as the heavens, earth, sun and moon,] cannot receive their life-force directly from the actual "ten utterances" recorded in the Torah, for the life-force issuing directly from them is far greater than the capacity of the individual creatures.[18] They can receive the life-force only when it descends and is progressively diminished, degree by degree, by means of substitutions and transpositions of the letters, and by means of *gematriot*, their numerical values,[19] until [the life-force] can be condensed and clothed, and a particular creature can be brought forth from it.

And the name by which [the creature] is called in the Holy Tongue is a vessel for the life-force condensed into the letters of that name which has descended from the "ten utterances" recorded in the Torah, that have the power and vitality to create a being *ex nihilo* and give it life forever. For "the Torah and the Holy One, blessed be He, are one."[20]

---

16. Ch. 2:4-5.

17. The Holy Tongue, the Hebrew of the Torah, was the language used in creation. Thus, all created things are directly affected by their Hebrew names, as well as by the component letters of their names. In this, the Holy Tongue is unlike other, arbitrary languages, the meaning of whose words is the result of mere consensus.

שֶׁכָּתוּב בְּסֵפֶר יְצִירָה, עַד שֶׁמִּשְׁתַּלְשֵׁל מֵעֲשָׂרָה מַאֲמָרוֹת וְנִמְשָׁךְ מֵהֶן צֵירוּף שֵׁם אֶבֶן, וְהוּא חַיּוּתוֹ שֶׁל הָאֶבֶן.

וְכֵן בְּכָל הַנִּבְרָאִים שֶׁבָּעוֹלָם, הַשֵּׁמוֹת שֶׁנִּקְרָאִים בָּהֶם בִּלְשׁוֹן הַקֹּדֶשׁ הֵן הֵן אוֹתִיּוֹת הַדִּבּוּר הַמִּשְׁתַּלְשְׁלוֹת מִמַּדְרֵגָה לְמַדְרֵגָה מֵעֲשָׂרָה מַאֲמָרוֹת שֶׁבַּתּוֹרָה, עַל יְדֵי חִילוּפִים וּתְמוּרוֹת הָאוֹתִיּוֹת בְּרל״א שְׁעָרִים, עַד שֶׁמַּגִּיעוֹת וּמִתְלַבְּשׁוֹת בְּאוֹתוֹ נִבְרָא לְהַחֲיוֹתוֹ.

לְפִי שֶׁאֵין פְּרָטֵי הַנִּבְרָאִים יְכוֹלִים לְקַבֵּל חַיּוּתָם מֵעֲשָׂרָה מַאֲמָרוֹת עַצְמָן שֶׁבַּתּוֹרָה, שֶׁהַחַיּוּת הַנִּמְשָׁךְ מֵהֶן עַצְמָן גָּדוֹל מְאֹד מִבְּחִינַת הַנִּבְרָאִים פְּרָטִיִּים, וְאֵין כֹּחַ בָּהֶם לְקַבֵּל הַחַיּוּת אֶלָּא עַל יְדֵי שֶׁיּוֹרֵד הַחַיּוּת וּמִשְׁתַּלְשֵׁל מִמַּדְרֵגָה לְמַדְרֵגָה פְּחוּתָה מִמֶּנָּה, עַל יְדֵי חִילוּפִים וּתְמוּרוֹת הָאוֹתִיּוֹת וְגִימַטְרִיָּאוֹת, שֶׁהֵן חֶשְׁבּוֹן הָאוֹתִיּוֹת, עַד שֶׁיּוּכַל לְהִתְצַמְצֵם וּלְהִתְלַבֵּשׁ וּלְהִתְהַוּוֹת מִמֶּנּוּ נִבְרָא פְּרָטִי.

וְזֶה שְׁמוֹ אֲשֶׁר יִקְרְאוּ לוֹ בִּלְשׁוֹן הַקֹּדֶשׁ הוּא כְּלִי לְחַיּוּת הַמְצוּמְצָם בְּאוֹתִיּוֹת שֵׁם זֶה שֶׁנִּשְׁתַּלְשֵׁל מֵעֲשָׂרָה מַאֲמָרוֹת שֶׁבַּתּוֹרָה, שֶׁיֵּשׁ בָּהֶם כֹּחַ וְחַיּוּת לִבְרוֹא יֵשׁ מֵאַיִן וּלְהַחֲיוֹתוֹ לְעוֹלָם, דְּאוֹרַיְיתָא וְקוּדְשָׁא בְּרִיךְ הוּא כּוֹלָא חַד.

---

18. I.e., it is far too intense to serve as their life-force.

19. The life-force may be so muted that it reaches a created being not even through a transposition of letters, but merely through their numerical equivalent.

20. Cf. *Zohar* I:24a; II:60a. I.e., just as G-d has the ability to create *ex nihilo*, so too do the "ten utterances" of the Torah.

Chapter 12

[Although there are only twenty-two letters,[21] they are able to create a vast multitude of creatures,] for the creatures are divided into categories [both] general[22] and particular.[23] [This multitudinous division comes about] by changes in the combinations, substitutions and transpositions [of the letters], as was explained above[24]—for every letter is a flow from an individual, particular life-force and power.[25]

And when many letters[26] are combined to form a word, then in addition to the numerous kinds of powers and life-forces which issue forth according to the number of letters in the word, there is, in addition, transcending all [the particular powers], the flow of a higher power and general life-force which contains and is equivalent to all the various individual powers and life-forces of the letters and transcends them all; it unites them and combines them,[27] in order to grant power and life-force to the world which was created, in [both] its general and particular aspects,[28] through this word.

---

21. The letters that constitute the "ten utterances," as Rabbi Schneur Zalman explained in earlier chapters, are effluences of the Divine attributes which are wholly united with G-d Himself. Therefore, though they are termed mere "letters," they are able to serve as vehicles for creating the wisdom and intellect of created beings, to which they are thus far superior; they are termed "letters" only in relation to the supernal attributes from which they emanate.

These letters are the specifically twenty-two manners of manifestation through which G-d chose to create the world. Accordingly, as the Rebbe, Rabbi Menachem M. Schneerson, notes, this chapter underscores the fact that all created beings, in all their vastly differentiated multiplicity, are in fact no more than twenty-two distinct forms of Divine manifestation. Moreover, continues the Rebbe, we can understand why Rabbi Schneur Zalman explains this concept at such length further on in this chapter. Such an explanation would seem to be at home in tracts such as *Sefer Yetzirah*, that deal with the respective stages of the creative process, not in a treatise dedicated to an explanation of Divine *Unity*. Rabbi Schneur Zalman explains this here, nevertheless, thereby actually highlighting the concept of Divine Unity—not only insofar as it exists in its Source, but as it exists in practice. For all the multifarious components of creation are in reality no more than twenty-two different forms of Divine manifestation.

פרק י"ב

רַק שֶׁהַבְּרוּאִים מִתְחַלְּקִים לְמִינֵיהֶם בִּכְלָלוּת וּבִפְרָטוּת עַל יְדֵי שִׁנּוּיֵי הַצֵּירוּפִים וְחִילוּפִים וּתְמוּרוֹת, כְּנִזְכָּר לְעֵיל, כִּי כָּל אוֹת הִיא הַמְשָׁכַת חַיּוּת וְכֹחַ מְיוּחָד פְּרָטִי.

וּכְשֶׁנִּצְטָרְפוּ אוֹתִיּוֹת הַרְבֵּה לִהְיוֹת תֵּיבָה, אֲזַי מִלְּבַד רִבּוּי מִינֵי כֹחוֹת וְחַיּוּת הַנִּמְשָׁכִים כְּפִי מִסְפַּר הָאוֹתִיּוֹת שֶׁבַּתֵּיבָה, עוֹד זֹאת הָעוֹלָה עַל כּוּלָּנָה הַמְשָׁכַת כֹּחַ עֶלְיוֹן וְחַיּוּת כְּלָלִית הַכּוֹלֶלֶת וּשְׁקוּלָה כְּנֶגֶד כָּל מִינֵי הַכֹּחוֹת וְהַחַיּוּת פְּרָטִיּוֹת שֶׁל הָאוֹתִיּוֹת וְעוֹלָה עַל גַּבֵּיהֶן, וְהִיא מְחַבַּרְתָּן וּמְצָרַפְתָּן יַחַד לְהַשְׁפִּיעַ כֹּחַ וְחַיּוּת לָעוֹלָם הַנִּבְרָא בְּתֵיבָה זוֹ לִכְלָלוֹ וְלִפְרָטָיו.

---

22. E.g., whether human or animal.

23. E.g., the animal world in turn comprises numerous species of beasts, birds, fish, etc.

24. When the letters are combined in one way, one kind of creature is created; a different combination gives rise to a different kind of creature. For as explained in ch. 1, certain letters may sometimes be substituted or transposed with others. Those creatures whose names are not mentioned in the "ten utterances" derive their vitality by means of the combinations, substitutions and transpositions of the letters that do appear in the "ten utterances."

25. **Since the letters are separate from each other, what combines them, and how is this accomplished?**

Rabbi Schneur Zalman now addresses this question.

26. I.e., many particular powers and life-forces.

27. **The root here translated "unites" (חבר) is etymologically related to the Hebrew word for "friend"; i.e., previously separate powers are joined in (as it were) friendly kinship. By contrast, the root here translated "combined" (צרף) means that these powers fuse into one created being and one word. In *Chagigah* 20b, *Rashi* likewise explains this verb to mean that a number of separate items "become one entity," and not merely similar to one entity. This widespread understanding of the verb also finds practical, legal application.**

28. I.e., with its individual created beings.

NOTE: Inasmuch as every single one of the twenty-two letters of the Torah is a flow of an individual, particular life-force and power, which does not flow through any other letter, therefore the written shape of each letter is likewise specific and distinctive, which indicates the pattern of the flow and manifestation of the light and life-force and power which is revealed and flows through this letter—[i.e.,] how it flows and is revealed from the attributes of the Holy One, blessed be He, and His will and His wisdom, and so on.[29]

As, for example, through the words of the utterance, *Let there be a firmament...*,[30] the seven heavens and all their component celestial hosts were created. Thus, our Sages, of blessed memory, speak of[31] [the firmament called] *Shechakim*, in which stand millstones that grind manna for the *tzaddikim*..., [the firmament called] *Zvul*, in which stand [the heavenly] Jerusalem and the Holy Temple and the Altar..., [and the firmament called] *Machon*, in which there are stores of snow and stores of hail...."[32]

The heavens as a whole were created and live and exist through the aggregate words of the utterance, *Let there be a firmament...*,[33] and each individual created being in the seven heavens[34] was created and lives and exists by virtue of some combination of the letters of these words, or their substitutions and transpositions, [these combinations, substitutions and transpositions being] according to the quality of the life-force of that particular creature. For every change in a combination is an intermixing and interweaving of the powers and life-forces in a different form,[35] since each letter

---

29. Returning to the body of the text, Rabbi Schneur Zalman now proceeds to illustrate how one utterance (*Let there be a firmament*) created the extensive components of the worlds as well as their specific creatures.

This also helps us understand the degree to which Divine Unity may be perceived in relation to the created beings of this world too, in that the seven heavens and all their ce-lestial hosts were created and live and exist from the solitary utterance, *Let there be a firmament.*

30. Genesis 1:6.

31. *Chagigah* 12b. See Commentary of the Rebbe at the conclusion of this chapter (*Lessons in Tanya*, vol. 3, p. 993-4).

הַגָּהָה: וּלְפִי שֶׁכָּל אוֹת וְאוֹת מִכּ"ב אוֹתִיּוֹת הַתּוֹרָה הִיא הַמְשָׁכַת חַיּוּת וְכֹחַ מְיֻחָד פְּרָטִי שֶׁאֵינוֹ נִמְשָׁךְ בְּאוֹת אַחֶרֶת, לְכָךְ גַּם תְּמוּנָתָן בִּכְתָב כָּל אוֹת הִיא בִּתְמוּנָה מְיֻחֶדֶת פְּרָטִית, הַמּוֹרָה עַל צִיּוּר הַהַמְשָׁכָה וְהִתְגַּלּוּת הָאוֹר וְהַחַיּוּת וְהַכֹּחַ הַנִּגְלָה וְנִמְשָׁךְ בְּאוֹת זוֹ, אֵיךְ הוּא נִמְשָׁךְ וְנִתְגַּלֶּה מִמִּדּוֹתָיו שֶׁל הַקָּדוֹשׁ בָּרוּךְ הוּא וּרְצוֹנוֹ וְחָכְמָתוֹ וְכוּ'.

כְּגוֹן, דֶּרֶךְ מָשָׁל, בַּתֵּיבוֹת שֶׁבְּמַאֲמַר יְהִי רָקִיעַ וְגוּ', שֶׁנִּבְרְאוּ בָּהֶן ז' רְקִיעִים וְכָל צְבָא הַשָּׁמַיִם אֲשֶׁר בָּהֶם, כְּמַאֲמַר רַבּוֹתֵינוּ זִכְרוֹנָם לִבְרָכָה שְׁחָקִים שֶׁבּוֹ רֵחַיִם עוֹמְדוֹת וְטוֹחֲנוֹת מָן לַצַּדִּיקִים וְכוּ', זְבוּל שֶׁבּוֹ יְרוּשָׁלַיִם וּבֵית הַמִּקְדָּשׁ וּמִזְבֵּחַ וְכוּ', מָכוֹן שֶׁבּוֹ אוֹצְרוֹת שֶׁלֶג וְאוֹצְרוֹת בָּרָד וְכוּ'.

שֶׁכְּלָלוּת הָרְקִיעִים נִבְרְאוּ וְחַיִּים וְקַיָּימִים בִּכְלָלוּת תֵּיבוֹת אֵלּוּ שֶׁבְּמַאֲמַר יְהִי רָקִיעַ וְכוּ', וּפְרָטֵי הַבְּרוּאִים שֶׁבְּז' רְקִיעִים, נִבְרָא כָּל פְּרָט מֵהֶם וְחַי וְקַיָּים מֵאֵיזֶה צֵירוּף אוֹתִיּוֹת מִתֵּיבוֹת אֵלּוּ, אוֹ חִילּוּפֵיהֶן וּתְמוּרוֹתֵיהֶן, שֶׁהֵן כְּפִי בְּחִינַת חַיּוּת הַנִּבְרָא הַפְּרָטִי הַהוּא. כִּי כָּל שִׁינּוּי צֵירוּף הוּא הַרְכָּבַת

---

32. Each of the seven firmaments thus has its general nature—the fact that it is a firmament—as well as its individual aspect, as exemplified above.

33. In general terms, their existence as heavens results from the comprehensive illumination contained within the words, *Let there be a firmament....*

Rabbi Schneur Zalman writes here that "the heavens *as a whole* were created...through the...words... *Let there be a firmament*," because each individual heaven was created by the name it is known by in the Holy Tongue (e.g., *Shechakim*), as stated above at the end of ch. 1.

34. **This includes the firmament itself, as explained above.**

35. For example: the three Hebrew letters א-ב-ן in that particular order comprise the word אבן, which is the name and life-force of a stone. When, however, these selfsame letters are transposed, a different form of creative power and life-force—and consequently a different creature—comes into being.

antecedent in the combination dominates and it is the essential [force] in this created being,[36] while the others [i.e., the other letters and forces contained within the word] are subordinate to it and are included in its light,[37] and thereby [through the different combinations of the same letters] a new being is created.

Likewise, through the substitution of letters or their transpositions,[38] new creatures are created that are of lower levels than the beings created from the [original] letters themselves. For they [the substituted letters], by way of illustration, resemble the light that shines upon the earth at night from the moon—and the moonlight is from the sun—hence, the light which is on the earth is a light [reflected] from the light of the sun.

Exactly so, allegorically speaking, the letters comprising the utterances are the aggregate flow of the life-force and the light and the power [that issue] from the attributes of the Holy one, blessed be He, to create the worlds from nothingness and to give them life and sustain them as long as such shall be His blessed will.[39] From this aggregate flow and mighty radiation of the utterances themselves, G-d caused its similar derivations and its offshoots to shine and issue forth, these being derivations and effluences of the light from the letters. And these [derivations and offshoots] are the substitutions of letters and their transpositions, with which He created the particular creatures of each world.

Likewise, G-d projected the light from the letters in another manner, and caused a radiation of a radiation of a radiation to issue forth and descend from the diffusions of light from the letters;[40] and likewise He further caused [the radia-

---

36. Since, for example, *alef* is the first letter of the word אבן, it is the dominant force in the created being that bears this name. If it is a letter stemming from the attribute of *chesed* (kindness), then that attribute will predominate; if it is a letter of *gevurah* (severity), a different attribute will prevail.

37. **This dominance of the initial letter of a word underlies the significance of *rashei tevot*, the pattern of abbreviation wherein a whole**

וַאֲרִיגַת הַכּוֹחוֹת וְהַחַיּוּת בְּשִׁינוּי, שֶׁכָּל אוֹת הַקּוֹדֶמֶת בְּצֵירוּף הִיא הַגּוֹבֶרֶת וְהִיא הָעִיקָר בִּבְרִיאָה זוֹ, וְהַשְּׁאָר טְפֵילוֹת אֵלֶיהָ וְנִכְלָלוֹת בְּאוֹרָהּ, וְעַל יְדֵי זֶה נִבְרֵאת בְּרִיָּה חֲדָשָׁה.

וְכֵן בְּחִילּוּפֵי אוֹתִיּוֹת אוֹ תְּמוּרוֹתֵיהֶן, נִבְרָאוֹת בְּרִיאוֹת חֲדָשׁוֹת פְּחוּתֵי הַמַּעֲלָה בְּעֵרֶךְ הַנִּבְרָאִים מֵהָאוֹתִיּוֹת עַצְמָן, כִּי הֵן דֶּרֶךְ מָשָׁל דּוּגְמַת אוֹר הַמֵּאִיר בַּלַּיְלָה בָּאָרֶץ מִן הַיָּרֵחַ, וְאוֹר הַיָּרֵחַ הוּא מֵהַשֶּׁמֶשׁ, וְנִמְצָא אוֹר שֶׁעַל הָאָרֶץ הוּא אוֹר הָאוֹר שֶׁל הַשֶּׁמֶשׁ.

וְכָכָה מַמָּשׁ, דֶּרֶךְ מָשָׁל, הָאוֹתִיּוֹת שֶׁבַּמַּאֲמָרוֹת הֵן כְּלָלוּת הַמְשָׁכַת הַחַיּוּת וְהָאוֹר וְהַכֹּחַ מִמִּדּוֹתָיו שֶׁל הַקָּדוֹשׁ בָּרוּךְ הוּא, לִבְרוֹא הָעוֹלָמוֹת מֵאַיִן לְיֵשׁ וּלְהַחֲיוֹתָן וּלְקַיְּימָן כָּל זְמַן מֶשֶׁךְ רְצוֹנוֹ יִתְבָּרֵךְ, וּמִכְּלָלוּת הַמְשָׁכָה וְהָאָרָה גְדוֹלָה הַזּוֹ, הֵאִיר ה' וְהִמְשִׁיךְ מִמֶּנָּה תוֹלְדוֹתֵיהָ כַּיּוֹצֵא בָהּ וַעֲנָפֶיהָ, שֶׁהֵן תּוֹלָדוֹת וְהַמְשָׁכַת הָאוֹר מֵהָאוֹתִיּוֹת, וְהֵן הֵן חִילּוּפֵי אוֹתִיּוֹת וּתְמוּרוֹתֵיהֶן, וּבָרָא בָהֶן בְּרוּאִים פְּרָטִים שֶׁבְּכָל עוֹלָם.

וְכֵן הֵאִיר ה' עוֹד, וְהִמְשִׁיךְ וְהוֹרִיד הֶאָרָה דְהֶאָרָה דְהֶאָרָה מֵהֶאָרוֹת הָאוֹתִיּוֹת, וְכֵן הִמְשִׁיךְ עוֹד וְהוֹרִיד עַד

---

word is telescoped within its first letter. Indeed, the Talmud states
(*Shabbat* 105a) that such abbrevia-
tions are of Torah origin.

38. When, for example, not only is
the order of the letters changed but
an *alef* (say) is substituted for an *ayin*.

39. The general life-force thus em-

anates from the utterances themselves.

40. In the earlier analogy, the moon's
reflected light was a radiation of the
sun's radiation. Rabbi Schneur Zalman now speaks of a descent one generation further removed—merely a
radiation of a radiation of a radiation.

tion of the radiation, etc.] to issue forth and descend to the lowest level in the chain of descents, until completely inanimate beings, such as stones and earth, were created. And their names אבן and עפר [the names being each object's life-force, as mentioned in ch. 1] are substitutions of substitutions, etc., and transpositions of transpositions, etc., as mentioned above.[41]

---

41. Thus, the life-force and existence of every created being are the letters of a particular Divine utterance, and to this the created being is utterly nul-

לְמַטָּה מַטָּה בִּבְחִינַת הִשְׁתַּלְשְׁלוּת, עַד שֶׁנִּבְרָא הַדּוֹמֵם מַמָּשׁ
כַּאֲבָנִים וְעָפָר, וּשְׁמוֹתֵיהֶן אֶבֶן וְעָפָר הֵם חִילוּפִים דְּחִילוּפִים
כו׳ וּתְמוּרוֹת דִּתְמוּרוֹת כו׳, כִּנְזְכָּר לְעֵיל.

—◆►◄◆—

APPENDIX II

CREATION VS. SPLITTING OF THE SEA
Excerpt from *Shaar Hayichud Veha'emunah*, Chapter 2

This [creation *ex nihilo*] is [even] more wondrous than, for example, the splitting of the Red Sea.[1] For then, G-d drove back the sea by a strong east wind all the night,[2] and the waters were split and [not merely ceased their flow, but] stood upright as a wall.

If G-d had stopped the wind, the waters would have instantly flowed downward, as is their way and nature, and undoubtedly they would not have stood upright like a wall, even though this nature of water [to flow downward] is also newly created *ex nihilo*[3]—for a stone wall stands erect by itself without [the assistance of] the wind, but the nature of water is not so.[4]

How much more so is it in the creation of something out of nothing, which transcends nature, and is far more miraculous than the splitting of the Red Sea, that surely with the withdrawal of the power of the Creator from the thing created, G-d forbid, the created being would revert to naught and utter non-existence.

---

1. Exodus 14:21-22; 15:8.

2. I.e., the G-dly force that split the sea vested itself in the wind.

3. As the Lubavitcher Rebbe points out, Rabbi Schneur Zalman means to say that not only is water itself a creation *ex nihilo,* but the nature of water to flow downward is also created *ex nihilo.*

When the mighty wind caused the water to stand like a wall, nothing was newly created *ex nihilo, yesh me'ayin;* this was no more than a case of *yesh me'yesh:* one existent state (the fluidity of water) was merely replaced by another existent state (its ability to remain upright).

Nevertheless, since the ability of water to stand rock-like is something novel, the force that is responsible for this novelty—even though this novelty involves no more than a progression from one *yesh* to another—must constantly cause it to come about; the moment it ceases to do so the novel event is arrested.

We thus see that the fluidity of water is not intrinsic to its essence. (By way of contrast, the fact that a created being occupies space, for example, is

הוספה ב

קטע משער היחוד והאמונה, פרק ב

וְהוּא פֶּלֶא גָּדוֹל יוֹתֵר מִקְּרִיעַת יַם סוּף, עַל דֶּרֶךְ מָשָׁל, שֶׁהוֹלִיךְ ה' אֶת הַיָּם בְּרוּחַ קָדִים עַזָּה כָּל הַלַּיְלָה, וַיִּבָּקְעוּ הַמַּיִם וְנִצְּבוּ כְמוֹ נֵד וְכַחוֹמָה.

וְאִילוּ הִפְסִיק ה' אֶת הָרוּחַ כְּרֶגַע, הָיוּ הַמַּיִם חוֹזְרִים וְנִיגָּרִים בְּמוֹרָד כְּדַרְכָּם וְטִבְעָם, וְלֹא קָמוּ כַחוֹמָה בְּלִי סָפֵק, אַף שֶׁהַטֶּבַע הַזֶּה בַּמַּיִם גַּם כֵּן נִבְרָא וּמְחוּדָּשׁ יֵשׁ מֵאַיִן, שֶׁהֲרֵי חוֹמַת אֲבָנִים נִצֶּבֶת מֵעַצְמָהּ בְּלִי רוּחַ, רַק שֶׁטֶּבַע הַמַּיִם אֵינוֹ כֵן.

וְכָל שֶׁכֵּן וְקַל וָחוֹמֶר בִּבְרִיאַת יֵשׁ מֵאַיִן, שֶׁהִיא לְמַעְלָה מֵהַטֶּבַע, וְהַפְלֵא וָפֶלֶא יוֹתֵר מִקְּרִיעַת יַם סוּף, עַל אַחַת כַּמָּה וְכַמָּה שֶׁבְּהִסְתַּלְּקוּת כֹּחַ הַבּוֹרֵא מִן הַנִּבְרָא חַס וְשָׁלוֹם, יָשׁוּב הַנִּבְרָא לְאַיִן וְאֶפֶס מַמָּשׁ.

---

an essential characteristic that does not require separate creation *ex nihilo*.) In order for water to be fluid a distinct act of creation *ex nihilo* is required.

Rabbi Schneur Zalman makes this point by citing the contrasting case of a stone wall, which stands upright, independently of any external force.

4. Since water by nature does not stand upright but flows downward, an additional degree of creation *ex nihilo* is called for if it is to do otherwise.

The above demonstrates that the Divine force that vested itself in the wind did not have to create *yesh me'ayin,* a newly existent being within creation: it merely had to change one *yesh* to another *yesh,* one form of existence to another—the natural property of fluidity to the natural property of standing erect. Nevertheless, even in such a situation, since a radical degree of change *is* involved, it is necessary for the power causing the change to effect the change unremittingly.

Surely, then, Rabbi Schneur Zalman soon concludes, with regard to the creation of the world, which comes into being absolutely *ex nihilo,* the activating force of the Creator must continuously be present in the created universe, providing it with life and existence. Indeed, were it not to be constantly present, the universe would revert to absolute nothingness.

Rather,[5] the activating force of the Creator must continuously be present in the thing created to give it life and existence.

[Activating forces such as the above] are the selfsame letters of speech [that constitute] the "ten utterances" by which [all beings] were created.[6]

---

5. Cf. *Kuzari* III:11.

6. This is why the above-quoted verse

states (Psalms 119:89), *Forever, O G-d, Your **word** stands in the heavens.* G-d's speech, which is the force that

אֶלָּא צָרִיךְ לִהְיוֹת כֹּחַ הַפּוֹעֵל בַּנִפְעָל תָּמִיד לְהַחֲיוֹתוֹ
וּלְקַיְּמוֹ.

וְהֵן הֵן בְּחִינַת אוֹתִיּוֹת הַדִּבּוּר מֵעֲשָׂרָה מַאֲמָרוֹת שֶׁבָּהֶם
נִבְרְאוּ.

—————◆❯◯❮◆—————

brings a created being into existence,   give it life and existence.
must be present there forever, so as to

APPENDIX III

MALCHUT AND THE OTHER SEFIROT

In the discourse entitled *Zeh Hayom 5741* (*Sefer Hamaamarim Melukat*, vol. 2, p. 107), the Lubavitcher Rebbe sums up the difference between *malchut* and the other *sefirot* by citing his father-in-law's discourse, *Shofar shel Rosh Hashanah 5699*[1]:

Malchut is different from all other attributes in its source, in its essence, in the manner of its essence, in its awakening and the manner of its awakening, in its revelation and the manner of its revelation.

In its source: All of the attributes are included in *arich anpin*,[2] while *malchut* stems from *radl'a*[3] (an acronym for *Reisha d'lo it'yada*—the beginning that is not known).

In its essence and the manner of its essence: All of the attributes, even as they exist in their source, *arich*, are in a state of "nine lights," whereas *malchut* is only a point and is in a state of non-being.

In its awakening and the manner of its awakening and its revelation: All of the attributes can be awakened of their own accord. The manner of their awakening can therefore be even from beings that are not in their realm. Their revelation can also be upon beings that are not in their realm at all. *Malchut*, by contrast, can be awakened only by another being. The manner of its awakening is therefore only from a being in its own realm; and its revelation is only upon one of its own realm.

In the manner of its revelation: The revelation of all of the attributes occurs in a manner of closeness. (E.g., the revelation of the attribute of *chesed*, kindness, occurs because of a

---

1. *Sefer Hamaamarim 5699*, p. 20.

2. ARICH ANPIN. The "outer," or lower, dimension of *Keter* (see above, footnote 161 to main text).

3. RADL'A. A Kabbalistic term indicating the deepest and innermost level of the Essence of G-d which is entirely unknowable—not only because of its profundity, but because it

feeling of closeness between the giver and the receiver. So it is with all of the attributes. Even the attribute of *gevurah*, severity, occurs because of a feeling of closeness.)

The revelation of *malchut*, by contrast, occurs in a manner of distance and separation, exaltedness and loftiness.

All of these distinctions stem from their distinction in source. Because *malchut* is rooted in *radl'a*—which is not only "the beginning that is unknown," it is also "the beginning that does not know [itself]"—it remains in a state of nonbeing even when it is drawn forth (its essence and the manner of its essence). And its awakening can occur only through another being. And the manner of its awakening and revelation must involve one of its realm.

In other words, all of the other attributes, because the essence of the attribute and its awakening stems from the person himself, such as the attribute of kindness or mercy, which (even their animation) are possible without the presence of another, the nature of the recipient of their kindness or mercy is therefore not critical. They can be awakened even by animals, although they are not in the human realm.

Malchut, on the other hand, because it comes only from the other, the other (i.e., the one who awakens the *malchut* and upon whom the *malchut* is revealed) must be of the same realm. Kingship is only possible upon humans, not on animals. Also, the other must be separate; one cannot be king over one's own children, for example.

The Rebbe goes on to clarify that in fact all of the attributes stem from *radl'a*. However, the purpose of the other attributes is revelation. Therefore, when they descend from *radl'a* and enter *arich* they become "lights." *Malchut*, on the other hand, even as it descends into the lower worlds, retains its nature as it is in *radl'a*.

---

is utterly beyond the realm of knowledge. Chasidus recognizes the bounds of intellect as innate. Intellect is a manifestation, a "power" of the soul or a *sefirah* of G-d, and is not Essence. Essence in turn transcends intellect. The *Ein Sof* is beyond knowledge because knowledge itself originates on a lower plane than G-d's Essence.

BIBLIOGRAPHY

BIBLIOGRAPHY

Ateret Rosh: Chasidic exposition of Rosh Hashanah, Yom Kippur, the Ten Days of Penintence and Shabbat Shuvah by Rabbi DovBer, second Lubavitcher Rebbe. Kopust, 1821; Shanghai, 1947; Revised Edition, Brooklyn, NY, 1989. (Heb.)

Avot: "Ethics of the Fathers." Talmudic tractate discussing moral and ethical teachings.

Bachya (or Bachaya): Commentary on the Torah by Rabbenu Bachaya ben Asher of Saragossa, Spain, student of R. Shlomo ben Aderet (Rashba). Naples, 1492.

Bati Legani 5710: Discourse published by Rabbi Yosef Yitzchak Schneersohn, sixth Lubavitcher Rebbe, in honor of 10 Shevat 5710 (1950).

Bati Legani 5711: Discourse delivered by the Lubavitcher Rebbe, Rabbi Menachem M. Schneerson, on 10 Shevat 5711 (1951).

Bava Batra: Talmudic tractate discussing Talmudic tractate discussing certain monetary issues.

Bava Kama: Talmudic tractate discussing the laws of torts and damages.

Bava Metzia: Talmudic tractate discussing certain monetary laws.

Bayom Hashemini Atzeret 5689: Discourse published by Rabbi Yosef Yitzchak Schneersohn, sixth Lubavitcher Rebbe, on Shemini Atzeret 5689 (1928).

Be'er Hagolah: Commentary on the Agadic statements of Talmudic Sages, by R. Yehudah Lowe of Prague, also known as Maharal. Prague, 5358 (1598).

Berachot: Talmudic tractate discussing the laws of blessings and prayer.

Baraita: Tannaic teachings from after the close of the Mishnah. These include: *Mishnat R. Chiya, Mishnat R. Oshiyah, Mishnat R. Eliezer ben Yaakov, Mechilta d'Rabbi Yishmael, Otiyot d'Rabbi Akiva, Torat Kohanim (Sifra)* on Leviticus, *Sifri* on Numbers and Deuteronomy.

Bereishit Rabbah: See *Midrash Rabbah*.

Beshaah Shehikdimu 5672: Series of discourses delivered by Rabbi Shalom DovBer Schneersohn, fifth Lubavitcher Rebbe, during the years 5672-5676 (1912-1915), named for its opening phrase; three volumes. (Heb.)

Chagigah: Talmudic tractate discussing festival sacrifices in the Beit Hamikdash.

Chullin: Talmudic tractate discussing various laws of kosher and sacrifices.

Derech Mitzvotecha: Talmudic tractate discussing various laws of kosher and sacrifices.

Devarim Rabbah: See *Midrash Rabbah*.

Ein Yaakov: Popular work, representing a compilation of *Aggadic* passages from the Talmud, compiled by R. Yaakov ben Shlomo ibn Chaviv (d. 1516).

Eitz Chaim: A compilation of the Arizal's Kabbalistic teachings, by his primary disciple and exponent, R. Chaim Vital (1543-1620).

Emek Hamelech: Commentary on the *Zohar* and the writings of the Arizal by one of his disciples, R. Naftali Hertz Bachrach of Frankfurt. Amsterdam, 1648. Revised edition, Jerusalem, 2003.

Haggadah: Lit., "Narrative." Book containing the service at the Passover Seder.

Iggeret Hakodesh: Third part of *Tanya*; a selection of letters by dealing with such topics as charity, prayer, and the like.

Ibn Ezra: Commentary on the Torah by R. Avraham Ibn Ezra (1080-1164) of Spain, expert grammarian, philosopher, astronomer, mathematician, doctor and poet. Naples, 1488; Constantinople, 1522.

Kehilat Yaakov: Yaakov: Encyclopedia of Kabbalistic terms by Rabbi Yaakov Tzvi Yalish of Dinov, disciple of Rabbi Yaakov Yitzchak Horowitz, the Chozeh of Lublin. Lvov, 1870. (Heb.)

Ketubot: Talmudic tractate discussing marriage contracts.

Kilayim: Mishnaic tractate discussing forbidden mixtures or hybrids of seeds, animals, plants and cloths.

Kuzari: Important work on Jewish philosophy and theology, by R. Yehudah Halevi. Written as a dialogue between the king of the Khazars and a Jewish scholar. Originally in Arabic, translated into Hebrew by R. Yehudah ibn Tibbon. Constantinople, 1506.

Lessons in Tanya: Linear exposition and commentary on Tanya based on a popular weekly radio series in Yiddish by Rabbi Yosef Wineberg. Each of the lectures was examined and amended by the Lubavitcher Rebbe, Rabbi Menachem M. Schneerson. (Five volumes, Heb. / Eng.)

Likkutei Sichot: Edited talks by the Lubavitcher Rebbe, Rabbi Menachem M. Schneerson; thirty-nine volumes. (Heb. / Yid.)

Likkutei Torah by Arizal: Kabbalistic work on Scripture by R. Isaac Luria, known as the Arizal.

Likkutei Torah: A collection of discourses elucidating major themes of Leviticus, Numbers, Deuteronomy, Song of Songs, Pesach, Shavuot, the High Holidays and Sukkot according to Chasidic philosophy. Delivered by the founder of Chabad Chasidus, Rabbi Schneur Zalman of Liadi, they were published in 5608 (1848) by his grandson Rabbi Menachem Mendel Schneersohn, third Lubavitcher Rebbe, the "Tzemach Tzedek." (Heb.)

Maharzu: Commentary on *Midrash Rabbah* by Rabbi Zev Wolf Einhorn of Horodna, Poland (d. 1862), printed in the standard editions of the Midrash with commentaries. (Heb.)

Mechilta: The earliest commentary on the Book of Exodus, by the school of R. Yishmael (circa. 120 c.e.), often quoted in the Talmud. First printed in Constantinople, 1515.

Metzudot David: Commentary on the Prophets and the Writings begun by R. David Altschuler and completed by his son R. Yechiel Hillel (18th Century), based in general on the commentaries of *Rashi*, *Radak* and *Ibn Ezra*.

Midrash Rabbah: A major collection of homilies and commentaries on the Torah, attributed to R. Oshaya Rabbah (circa. 3rd century); some place it as a work of the early Gaonic period. This work covers the Five Books of Moses and the Five *Megillot*.

Midrash Tanchuma: Midrash on the Torah attributed to R. Tanchuma bar Abba, and compiled during the early centuries of the Common Era. Constantinople, 1522.

Mishnat Chasidim: A summary of the Arizal's wisdom concerning spiritual worlds, souls, and meditations by R. Immanuel Chai Ricci (1688-1743), rabbi and important Kabbalist in Italy.

Mystical Concepts in Chassidism: Guide to the intricate concepts of Jewish mysticism found in Chabad Chasidic philosophy. Authored by Rabbi J. Immanuel Schochet (Kehot, 1988). (Eng.)

Nehar Shalom: Commentary on R. Chaim Vital's *Eitz Chaim*, by the Kabbalist, R. Shalom Shar'abi, focusing on the concentrations and intentions of prayer and mitzvah performance. Warsaw, 5651 (1891).

Onkelos: Aramaic translation of the Torah authored by

Onkelus (2nd century c.e.), a proselyte of Roman origin, under the guidance of R. Eliezer and R. Yehoshua. Rashi (*Kiddushin* 49a, s.v. *harei zeh mecharef*) says of Onkelus, that he "did not add anything to the Torah, because it was all given at Mount Sinai. It was subsequently forgotten and he restated it, as recounted in Tractate *Megillah* (3a)."

Or Hatorah: Chasidic discourses and commentary on the Torah, Prophets, Writings, Talmud, Prayer and miscellaneous topics by Rabbi Menachem Mendel Schneersohn, third Lubavitcher Rebbe, the "Tzemach Tzedek"; forty-one volumes, Kehot. (Heb.)

Orchot Tzadikim: Lit., "Ways of the Righteous." Also called *Sefer Hamiddot* (Book of Traits), this a book on ethics written by an unknown author, first appearing in print in Prague, 1581. From the original title page: "This compilation, small in quantity but large in quality, is a book of the ways of the righteous and the traits of the soul. Established to teach and educate the foolish heart of stone, to pull it from the mud and mire, to lead it on the path of goodness which is without stumble. Man will then not be for iniquity, embarrassment or shame." It is a popular work in many circles to this day.

Otzrot Chaim: A compilation of the Arizal's Kabbalistic teachings, by his primary disciple and exponent, R. Chaim Vital (1543-1620).

Out of the Inferno: Vast collection of communications, letters and memoranda pertaining to the efforts that led to the rescue of Rabbi Yosef Yitzchak Schneerson, sixth Lubavitcher Rebbe from war-torn Europe in 1939-40 (Kehot 2002).

Pardes (Pardes Rimonim): Kabbalistic work by R. Moshe Cordovero (Ramak) of Safed (1522-1570), leader of a prominent Kabbalistic school in Safed.

Pesachim: Talmudic tractate discussing the Passover laws.

Pirkei d'Rabbi Eliezer: A Midrash authored by the second century Mishnaic Sage, R. Eliezer ben Horkenus, also known as R. Eliezer Hagadol ("the great"). "The earliest of all Tannaic treatises, revealed and famous in the era of our authoritative rabbis and mystical Kabbalists, the *Rishonim*, who used and benefited from its light" (from the title page).

Pesikta: A small book on the Festivals, containing Aphorisms of Talmudic Sages arranged similar to *Midrash Rabbah*. The *Yalkut Shimoni* quotes certain aphorisms from the *Pesikta*.

Pri Eitz Chaim: A compilation of the Arizal's mystical rituals pertaining to Prayer, recorded by R. Chaim Vital and arranged in the present order by the Kabbalist, R. Meir Popporos (1624-1662).

Radal: Commentary on *Pirkei d'Rabbi Eliezer* by R. Dovid Luria (1798-1855) of Bichov, Jewish leader in Lithuania. Warsaw, 1852.

Ramban: Commentary on the Torah by R. Moshe ben Nachman, or Nachmanides (1194-1270), Jewish leader in Gerona, Spain and later in the Land of Israel; prolific author of numerous major classics on the Bible, Talmud, Jewish law, Kabbalah, philosophy and medicine.

Ran: Rabbenu Nissim of Barcelona, Spain (1290-1375). Famous for his extensive commentary to *The Book of Laws* by R. Yitzchak Alfasi, known as the Rif, printed at the end of many Talmudic tractates. He also authored a collection of homiletic discourses discussing the essentials of Jewish faith, a partial commentary to the Torah and liturgical hymns.

Rashash: Commentary on *Midrash Rabbah* by Rabbi Shmuel Shtrashun of Vilna (1794-1872), first appearing in the Vilna edition of the Midrash in 1843-45 and 1855.

Rashi: Acronym for R. Shlomo Yitzchaki. R. Shlomo ben Yitzchak lived in Troyes, France and Worms, Germany (1040-1105). His commentary is printed in practically all editions of the Torah and Talmud, and is the subject of some two hundred commentators.

Rosh Hashanah: Talmudic tractate discussing the laws of the Rosh Hashanah festival and the Jewish calendar.

Rut Rabbah: See *Midrash Rabbah*.

Sanhedrin: Talmudic tractate discussing court justice and/or the Supreme Court in ancient Israel, consisting of 71 members.

Sefer Hachaim: An ethical work by R. Chaim ben Betzalel, brother of R. Yehudah Lowe (Maharal) of Prague. Cracow, 5353 (1593).

Sefer Halichot Eli: Rules and guidelines of the Talmud in order of the *alef-beit*. Also included are rules and guidelines of Maimonides and original Talmudic Torah thoughts. Authored by R. Shlomo Algazi and published in Izmir, 5435 (1675).

Sefer Halikkutim: Collection of concepts explained in Chasidic teachings, culled from the works by R. Menachem Mendel of Lubavitch, the "Tzemach Tzedek." Arranged in *alef-beit* form, it also contains references to the works of the other Chabad Rebbes for the respective topics. Twenty-two volumes.

Sefer Hapardes: Kabbalistic work by R. Moshe Cordovero (Ramak) of Safed (1522-1570). Leader of a prominent Kabbalistic school in Safed, Ramak is regarded as one of the most important and lucid expositors and systematists of Jewish Mysticism.

Sefer Hamaamarim 5643-5680: Set of Chasidic discourses delivered by Rabbi Shalom DovBer Schneersohn, fifth Lubavitcher Rebbe, between 5643-5680 (1883-1920), the years of his leadership; twenty-five volumes. (Heb.)

Sefer Hamaamarim 5680-5710: Set of Chasidic discourses delivered by Rabbi Yosef Yitzchak Schneersohn, sixth Lubavitcher Rebbe, between 5680-5710 (1920-1950), the years of his leadership; nineteen volumes. (Heb.)

Sefer Hamaamarim Kayitz 5700: Collection of Chasidic discourses delivered by Rabbi Yosef Yitzchak Schneersohn, sixth Lubavitcher Rebbe, between his arrival to the USA before Purim, 5700 (1940), and Rosh Hashanah, 5701.

Sefer Hamaamarim Melukat: Chasidic discourses delivered and edited by the Lubavitcher Rebbe, Rabbi Menachem M. Schneerson, during the course of his leadership 5711-5752 (1951-1992). Six volumes (Kehot, 1987-1992). (Heb.)

Sefer Yetzirah: One of the oldest written sources of Kabbalah, it is attributed to the Patriarch Abraham. It has been the subject of over one hundred commentaries since it was first published in Mantua, 1562.

Shaar Hakavanot: Kabbalistic explanation of the concentrations and intentions of prayer, mitzvah performance and Torah study; sixth of the eight *She'arim* ("Gates") by R. Chaim Vital. See *Eitz Chaim*.

Shaar Hayichud Veha'emunah: Second part of *Tanya*; explores the doctrines of Divine Unity, Providence and faith. Twelve chapters.

Shabbat: Talmudic tractate discussing the laws of Shabbat.

Shelah: Acronym for *Shnei Luchot Habrit*, a monumental work by R. Yeshaya Horowitz, (1558-1628), Chief Rabbi of Prague, containing explanations and commentaries on the profound aspects of the Torah, *mitzvot*, the festivals, Jewish customs and the fundamental beliefs of Judaism, including basic instruction in Kabbalah. First published in Amsterdam, 1648.

Shemot Rabbah: See *Midrash Rabbah*.

Shir Hashirim Rabbah: See *Midrash Rabbah*.

Shulchan Aruch Harav: Code of Jewish law by R. Schneur Zalman of Liadi. Shklov, 1814; Brooklyn, NY, 1960-8; New, Revised Edition, Brooklyn, 1999-2004.

Sotah: Talmudic tractate discussing the law of the suspected adulteress.

Taamei Hamitzvot: Kabbalistic work on the 613 commandments compiled by primary disciple and exponent of R. Yitzchak Luria's Kabbalistic teachings, R. Chaim Vital (1543-1620). (Heb.)

Taanit: Talmudic tractate discussing fast days.

Tanna d'Vei Eliyahu Rabbah: A Midrash taught by Elijah the Prophet to Rav Anan, an Amora, in two parts named Seder Eliyahu Rabbah and Seder Eliyahu Zutta. (See Kesubot 106a where this event is recorded.)

Tanya: Philosophical *magnum opus* by Rabbi Schneur Zalman of Liadi, in which the principles of Chabad are expounded. The name is derived from the initial word of this work. Also called *Likkutei Amarim*.

Targum Yonatan: An Aramaic translation/commentary on the Torah authored by Yonathan ben Uziel (circa 50 c.e.), a disciple of Hillel the Elder. The Talmud (*Megillah* 3b) relates that upon concluding his translation of the Prophets, a storm of criticism arose that rocked the land of Israel. A Heavenly voice rang out: "Who revealed My secrets to mankind?" Whereupon Yonathan ben Uziel arose and proclaimed, "It was I that revealed Your secrets. It is revealed and known before You that I did not do it for my own honor nor for that of my father's house, but for Your honor, in order that disputes should not multiply in Israel!" He wished to continue and translate the Writings too, but a Heavenly voice called out, "Enough!"

Tikkunei Zohar: A work of seventy chapters on the first word of the Torah, by the school of R. Shimon bar Yochai (circa. 120 c.e.). First printed in Mantua, 1558, *Tikkunei Zohar* contains some of the most important discussions in Kabbalah, and is essential for understanding the *Zohar*.

Torat Chaim: A collection of discourses elucidating major themes of the Torah portions of Bereishit-Pekudei, by Rabbi DovBer of Lubavitch. Kopust, 1886; Brooklyn NY, 1974; 2003.

Torat Shmuel 5633: Chasidic discourses delivered by R. Shmuel Schneersohn, fourth Lubavitcher Rebbe, during the year 5633 (1873).

Tosfot: A dialectic commentary on the Talmud, generally printed opposite the commentary of Rashi, largely the product of Rashi's students and grandsons (circa. 1100-1171).

The Four Worlds: English translation of a letter by R. Yosef Yitzchak Schneersohn, sixth Lubavitcher Rebbe, dated 15 Marcheshvan 5698 (1937) discussing the four worlds of *Atzilut, Beriah, Yetzirah* and *Asiyah* (Kehot, 2003).

Tur: Two works by this name were authored by R. Yaakov ben Asher. One, a code of Jewish law—also called *Arba'a Turim*—was first published in Piove di Sacco, 1475. The other, a commentary on the Torah, first appeared in Constantinople, 1514.

Vayikra Rabbah: See *Midrash Rabbah*.

Ve'avraham Zaken 5666: Discourse delivered by R. Shalom DovBer Schneersohn, fifth Lubavitcher Rebbe, on Shabbat *Chaye Sara* 5666 (1905).

Vera'iti Ani 5662: Discourse delivered by R. Shalom DovBer Schneersohn, fifth Lubavitcher Rebbe, on Shabbat *Matot-Massei* 5662 (1902).

Yalkut Reuveni: A compilation culled from discourses,

Midrashim and Kabbalistic works on the Torah, by R. Avraham Reuven Katz. Prague, 5420 (1660).

Yefei Toar: Commentary on Midrash Rabbah by R. Shmuel Yaffe Ashkenazi (c. 1525-1595), rabbi in Istanbul.

Yom Tov Shel Rosh Hashanah 5666: Series of discourses delivered by Rabbi Shalom DovBer Schneersohn, fifth Lubavitcher Rebbe, during the years 5666-7 (1905-7), named for its opening words.

Zohar: Lit. "radiance." Basic work of Kabbalah; compiled by Rabbi Shimon Bar Yochai (second century Mishnaic sage); written in Hebrew and Aramaic as a commentary on the Torah.

—◈►◄◈—

INDEX

INDEX

OTHER TITLES IN
THE CHASIDIC HERITAGE SERIES

THE ETERNAL BOND *from Torah Or*
By Rabbi Schneur Zalman of Liadi
Translated by Rabbi Ari Sollish
This discourse explores the spiritual significance of *brit milah*, analyzing two dimensions in which our connection with G-d may be realized. For in truth, there are two forms of spiritual circumcision: Initially, man must "circumcise his heart," freeing himself to the best of his ability from his negative, physical drives; ultimately, though, it is G-d who truly liberates man from his material attachment.

≼∘≼∘≼∘

JOURNEY OF THE SOUL from *Torah Or*
By Rabbi Schneur Zalman of Liadi
Translated by Rabbi Ari Sollish
Drawing upon the parallel between Queen Esther's impassioned plea to King Ahasuerus for salvation and the soul's entreaty to G-d for help in its spiritual struggle, this discourse examines the root of the soul's exile, and the dynamics by which it lifts itself from the grip of materiality and ultimately finds a voice with which to express its G-dly yearnings. Includes a brief biography of the author.

≼∘≼∘≼∘

TRANSFORMING THE INNER SELF from *Likkutei Torah*
By Rabbi Schneur Zalman of Liadi
Translated by Rabbi Chaim Zev Citron
This discourse presents a modern-day perspective on the Biblical command to offer animal sacrifices. Rabbi Schneur Zalman teaches that each of us possesses certain character traits that can be seen as "animalistic," or materialistic, in nature, which can lead a person toward a life of material indulgence. Our charge, then, is to "sacrifice" and transform the animal within, to refine our animal traits and utilize them in our pursuit of spiritual perfection.

≼∘≼∘≼∘

FLAMES from *Gates of Radiance*
By Rabbi DovBer of Lubavitch
Translated by Dr. Naftoli Loewenthal
This discourse focuses on the multiple images of the lamp, the oil, the wick and the different hues of the flame in order to express profound guidance in the divine service of every individual. Although *Flames* is a Chanukah discourse, at the same time, it presents concepts that are of perennial significance. Includes the first English biography of the author ever published.

৵৵৵

THE MITZVAH TO LOVE YOUR FELLOW AS YOUR-
SELF from *Derech Mitzvotecha*
By Rabbi Menachem Mendel of Lubavitch, the Tzemach Tzedek
Translated by Rabbis Nissan Mangel and Zalman I. Posner
The discourse discusses the Kabbalistic principle of the "collective soul of the world of *Tikkun*" and explores the essential unity of all souls. The discourse develops the idea that when we connect on a soul level, we can love our fellow as we love ourselves; for in truth, we are all one soul. Includes a brief biography of the author.

৵৵৵

TRUE EXISTENCE *Mi Chamocha 5629*
By Rabbi Shmuel of Lubavitch
Translated by Rabbis Yosef Marcus and Avraham D. Vaisfiche
This discourse revolutionizes the age-old notion of Monotheism, i.e., that there is no other god besides Him. Culling from Talmudic and Midrashic sources, the discourse makes the case that not only is there no other god besides Him, there is nothing besides Him—literally. The only thing that truly exists is G-d. Includes a brief biography of the author.

৵৵৵

TRUE EXISTENCE *The Chasidic View of Reality*
A Video-CD with Rabbi Manis Friedman
Venture beyond science and Kabbalah and discover the world of Chasidism. This Video-CD takes the viewer step-by-step through the basic chasidic and kabbalistic view of creation and existence. In clear, lucid language, Rabbi Manis Friedman deciphers these esoteric concepts and demonstrates their modern-day applications.

ৰ্জ-ৰ্জ-ৰ্জ

YOM TOV SHEL ROSH HASHANAH 5659
Discourse One
By Rabbi Shalom DovBer of Lubavitch
Translated by Rabbis Yosef Marcus and Moshe Miller
The discourse explores the attribute of *malchut* and the power of speech while introducing some of the basic concepts of Chasidism and Kabbalah in a relatively easy to follow format. Despite its title and date of inception, the discourse is germane throughout the year. Includes a brief biography of the author.

ৰ্জ-ৰ্জ-ৰ্জ

FORCES IN CREATION
Yom Tov Shel Rosh Hashanah 5659 Discourse Two
By Rabbi Shalom DovBer of Lubavitch
Translated by Rabbis Moshe Miller and Shmuel Marcus
This is a fascinating journey beyond the terrestrial, into the myriad spiritual realms that shape our existence. In this discourse, Rabbi Shalom DovBer systematically traces the origins of earth, Torah and souls, drawing the reader higher and higher into the mystical, cosmic dimensions that lie beyond the here and now, and granting a deeper awareness of who we are at our core.

ৰ্জ-ৰ্জ-ৰ্জ

THE POWER OF RETURN
Yom Tov Shel Rosh Hashanah 5659 Discourse Three
By Rabbi Shalom DovBer of Lubavitch
Translated by Rabbi Y. Eliezer Danzinger
In this discourse Rabbi Shalom DovBer examines of the inner workings of *teshuvah*, and explains how it is precisely through making a detailed and honest examination of one's character and spiritual standing—which inevitably leads one to a contrite and broken heart—that allows one to realize his or her essential connection with G-d.

∾∾∾

OVERCOMING FOLLY
Kuntres Umaayan Mibeit Hashem
By Rabbi Shalom DovBer of Lubavitch
Translated by Rabbi Zalman I. Posner
In this classis ethico-philosophical work, Rabbi Shalom DovBer weaves Chasidic doctrine, Kabbalah thoughts, Biblical and Talmudic texts and candid insights into human frailties into a document structured and systematic, yet informal and personal—a text for study and meditation.

∾∾∾

THE PRINCIPLES OF
EDUCATION AND GUIDANCE
Klalei Hachinuch Vehahadrachah
By Rabbi Yosef Yitzchak of Lubavitch
Translated by Rabbi Y. Eliezer Danzinger
The Principles of Education and Guidance is a compelling treatise that examines the art of educating. In this thought provoking analysis, Rabbi Yosef Yitzchak teaches how to assess the potential of any pupil, how to objectively evaluate one's own strengths, and how to successfully use reward and punishment—methods that will help one become a more effective educator.

∾∾∾

the soul burns forever. This discourse speaks to one who finds pleasure in the material world, yet struggles to find spirituality in his or her life.

৩৪৩৪৩৪

VICTORY OF LIGHT *Tanu Rabanan Mitzvat Ner Chanukah 5738*
By Rabbi Menachem M. Schneerson, the Lubavitcher Rebbe
Translated by Rabbi Yosef Marcus
Even darkness has a purpose: to be transformed into light. In this compelling discourse, the Lubavitcher Rebbe, Rabbi Menachem M. Schneerson, explains how we can draw strength from the story of Chanukah for our battle with spiritual darkness, so that we, like the Macabees of old, may attain a *Victory of Light.*

৩৪৩৪৩৪

ON THE ESSENCE OF CHASIDUS
Kuntres Inyana Shel Toras Hachasidus
By Rabbi Menachem M. Schneerson, the Lubavitcher Rebbe
In this landmark discourse, the Lubavitcher Rebbe, Rabbi Menachem M. Schneerson, explores the contribution of Chasidus to a far deeper and expanded understanding of Torah. The Rebbe analyzes the relationship Chasidus has with Kabbalah, the various dimensions of the soul, the concept of Moshiach and the Divine attributes—all in this slim volume.

৩৪৩৪৩৪

NURTURING FAITH *Kuntres Purim Kattan 5752*
By Rabbi Menachem M. Schneerson, the Lubavitcher Rebbe
Translated by Rabbi Yosef Marcus
At its core, this discourse discusses the function of a *nassi,* a Jewish leader, who awakens within every single person the deepest part of the soul. Similar to Moses, the *nassi* inspires the person so that one's most basic faith in G-d leaves the realm of the abstract and becomes real. *Nurturing Faith* will cultivate your bond with the Rebbe's role as the Moses of our generation.

৩৪৩৪৩৪

THERE ARE MANY IMPORTANT MANUSCRIPTS
THAT ARE READY TO GO TO PRESS, BUT ARE
WAITING FOR A SPONSOR LIKE YOU.

PLEASE CONSIDER ONE OF THESE OPPORTUNITIES
AND MAKE AN EVERLASTING CONTRIBUTION TO
JEWISH SCHOLARSHIP AND CHASIDIC LIFE.

FOR MORE INFORMATION PLEASE CONTACT:

THE CHASIDIC HERITAGE SERIES
770 EASTERN PARKWAY
BROOKLYN, NEW YORK 11213
TEL: 718.774.4000
E-MAIL: INFO@KEHOTONLINE.COM

COMING SOON!

LECHA DODI 5689 & 5714
By Rabbi Yosef Yitzchak of Lubavitch
and Rabbi Menachem M. Schneerson, the Lubavitcher Rebbe
Translated by Rabbi Ari Sollish

∾∾∾

UMIKNEH RAV 5666
By Rabbi Shalom DovBer of Lubavitch
Translated by Rabbi Yosef Marcus

∾∾∾

TRACT ON PRAYER *Kunteres Hatefillah*
By Rabbi Shalom DovBer of Lubavitch
Translated by Rabbi Y. Eliezer Danzinger

∾∾∾

הוצאת ספרים
כרתי הוד תורה
ליובאוויטש